Landscapes of
S**O**RRENTO
and the
AM**A**LFI COAST
a countryside guide

Julian Tippett

SUNFLOWER
BOOKS

First published 1996
by Sunflower Books
12 Kendrick Mews
London SW7 3HG, UK

ISBN 1-85691-067-9

Important note to the reader

We have tried to ensure that the descriptions and maps in this book are error-free at press date. The book will be updated, where necessary, whenever future printings permit. It will be very helpful for us to receive your comments (sent in care of the publishers, please) for the updating of future printings.

We also rely on those who use this book — especially walkers — to take along a good supply of common sense when they explore. If the route is not as we outline it here, and your way ahead is not secure, return to the point of departure. **Never attempt to complete a tour or walk under hazardous conditions!** Please read carefully the notes on pages 15 to 19, the Country code on page 136, and the introductory comments at the beginning of each walk segment. Explore **safely**, while at the same time respecting the beauty of the countryside.

This book differs slightly from other titles in the Landscapes Series. Originally published privately by the author as 'Walks from Amalfi', the book was so well received that we have preserved the original format of walk *segments and planners*, while at the same time expanding the area covered and adding several car tours and excursions.

With thanks to my wife, Pat, and to Antonio Calvano, for their encouragement

Cover: The descent to Santa Maria Maddalena, Atrani (Excursion 4, Walk segments 3 and 15)
Title page: Villa Cimbrone, Ravello
Above: Bell in the monastery of San Domenico (Walk segment 29)

Photographs and maps by the author
A CIP catalogue record for this book is available from the British Library.
Printed and bound in the UK by Brightsea Press, Exeter

10 9 8 7 6 5 4 3 2

Contents

Preface

The coastal towns south of Naples have attracted travellers for a hundred years and more, Wagner, Ibsen, Ruskin and Longfellow being amongst the more famous. Today visitors come in their thousands to stay in Sorrento or in small towns further along the coast, from where they visit Pompei, take a trip up Vesuvius or catch the ferry to Capri. They also come to soak up the sensational coastal scenery of soaring limestone cliffs, serpentine roads and clinging hillside villages. And they will spend time looking around the towns, drinking cappuccino in the bar of a small piazza, and perhaps relaxing by the pool. All the ingredients are in place for a leisurely Mediterranean holiday.

When you are ready to explore the area in depth, try one of the 'Excursions with picnic' suggested on pages 20-23; these are easy but attractive outings, ideal for hot or 'lazy' days. Or, if you are hiring a car, dip into the Touring section to get off the beaten track.

But if you like to walk, another ingredient will intrigue and tempt you. Accident of history and steepness of terrain have preserved a network of ancient footpaths which reaches from the towns into the surrounding countryside. These paths let you leave the bustle of town life and the clamour of motor traffic, to walk among lemon groves, visit hillside villages, see remote monasteries and, along the way, be regaled by the most stunning of views. The paths are often paved in stone or, if climbing the steep hillsides, consist of flights of steps. And the flowers are a constant delight: from broom and rosemary in March to freesias and cistus in May. In autumn, the woods are carpeted with cyclamen. So, if you are willing to put in a little effort, a whole new world awaits you.

Most of the paths described here can be followed easily by people who do not claim to be regular walkers, though committed hikers will like them just the same. The walks are described in such a way as to give many choices when planning an outing; that is, as well as deciding where to go, you can choose whether to be more or less energetic, and

whether to go for a shorter or longer walk. Besides being flexible, the path network is splendidly accessible. Often you can start walking directly from the door of your hotel, or, at most, a short bus journey is needed to reach the start of the walk. Just a few of the walks are for experts only, as you will see in the text.

A great beauty of walking when abroad is that you leave the ways preordained for tourists. Instead of meeting only people whose stock-in-trade is to deal with visitors, you come across farmers or others going about their daily lives. We (my wife and I) have met a craftsman intent on showing us his baskets made from split chestnut; a retired hotel porter who wanted to share a bottle of his surprisingly good home-made wine; a farmer harvesting grapes who insisted on replacing the shop-bought grapes we were eating on our picnic. And you come across other like-minded walkers with a sense of adventure. Meeting people one-to-one as you do on a footpath, you tend to get into conversation or, if your language skills are not up to it, there is at least mutual recognition, and especially so here, where the local people are so friendly and open. In short, you feel included in the life of the countryside. This splendid feeling, together with the marvellous sights all around, make for an unbeatable combination. I hope the foregoing is persuasive enough to tempt you into trying some of these walks, but beware, you may become hooked!

On the flower-filled descent to the Torre Damecuta, with Ischia beyond (Walk segment 72 on Capri)

Introduction

The guide has been designed as a reference book to dip into according to need. This first section deals with topics that apply to the whole region — defining and describing the region covered by the guide, local transport, food and drink, how to plan a holiday here, advice on walking the paths, notes on flora and fauna. It is followed by a short section, 'Excursions with picnic', to give ideas for some outings based on *bus travel* which will take you off the beaten track with a minimum of physical effort. These trips often follow sections (usually downhill) of the main walks. Another short section, 'Touring', offers similar ideas for excursions for *motorists*.

The major part of the book is devoted to *walks* from the six main tourist areas. Certainly one, but perhaps two or three of these sections will be of interest to you — depending on where you are staying and whether you wish sometimes to take a bus or a boat to walk outside your 'home' territory

The walks are not described as separate complete routes as is usual in *Landscapes* guides, but as *segments*, each of which is a connecting link in the path network. You make up your own routes by stringing segments together to build a walk of the desired length and difficulty; to help you, there is a 'walk planner' diagram for each of the six areas. Once you are on the walk, detailed instructions enable you to link together the segments you have chosen. This arrangement gives great flexibility for planning walks to suit every need and is possible only because the footpaths here happen to form a true network, *but it does require some attention to learn the rules*. The detail of how to plan a walk is described on page 17. You are urged to examine this explanation closely, to get the most out of this book.

Preceding the walks in each of the six areas there is other helpful information, such as a description of the terrain and any special transport arrangements. Town plans are included here, as well as a brief summary of the popular tourist sights. In general, however, this guide leaves the task of describing towns and historical sites to the many other publications so easily obtained near your hotel.

The Amalfi Peninsula

Sometimes also called the Sorrento Peninsula, this mountainous tongue of land forms the southern arm of the Bay of Naples, with Sorrento itself sitting near its tip on a shelf some 60 metres (200 feet) above the sea. The Lattari (derived from the Latin word for milk) mountains in the spine of the peninsula rise to 1440 metres (nearly 5000 feet), often presenting a majestic scene of great limestone cliffs and profound chasms. The world-famous Amalfi Coast occupies the southern edge of the peninsula and here lies that noted string of holiday resorts — Positano, Praiano, Amalfi, Minori and Maiori. All along the coastline the mountains rise steeply from the sea to make the tortuous road which connects the towns into the most exhilarating drive imaginable.

Of the famous towns of the region, the only one not located on the coast is Ravello, which sits in all its glory some 360 metres (1200 feet) high on an arm projecting south from the mountains, towering over the coastline nearby. Two high plains relieve the mountainous scene, Agerola and Tramonti, but otherwise the countryside is always either hilly or mountainous, perhaps being least steep behind Sorrento. Six kilometres off the tip of the peninsula lies the rocky island of Capri.

Looking west from the cemetery in Amalfi beyond the town to the hillside visited on Walk segment 9 and to Conca dei Marini on the skyline.

Typical cast-iron lampposts frame the view east along the coast from the small piazza by Santa Maria Maddalena in Atrani (Excursion 4, Walk segment 3).

Planning a holiday

Probably the easiest method of installing yourself in the region for a holiday, and possibly the cheapest, is to take a package tour which provides travel, transfers and hotel. With such a package and this book, you have a fine self-made walking or touring holiday. Check the location of the hotel in case it is some way out of town and would therefore entail a journey to get into the walking network. The principal operators from the UK in this region are: Citalia, Italian Escapades, Magic of Italy and Thomson Holidays (especially their Small & Friendly programme).

For the independent traveller, all towns have a selection of hotels and pensions, with reservations usually needed only in high season (mid July to mid September) and at Easter.

Getting about

These notes outline the basic principles of using buses, trains and boats *in the region,* and show how to transfer independently to your resort. Details of *local* transport are to be found in the area descriptions starting on page 34; bus timetables begin on page 128.

Bus services. The SITA company runs the out of town buses with a fleet of blue buses that operate reliably and punctually, the odd strike *(sciopero)* excepted. The drivers are much to be admired for their patient, calm and skilled driving, often when faced with great congestion on the tortuous and narrow coastal corniche road. Services are relatively frequent.

Bus stops carry the legend FERMATA SITA. If you are taking a walk or going on one of the suggested outings, the name for the bus stop where you alight is given in the text (unless it is simply the name of the village). If you are uncertain of knowing when you have reached your stop, ask the driver to drop you off using this phrase: 'Per favore, ci può far scendere alla fermata … (name of the stop)'.

8

A moody evening view of Capri and the Faraglione islands seen from Termini (Excursion 13; Tour 1, Walk segments 53, 58, 60, and 61)

You could even write this out to show him. The 'ci' means 'us'; if travelling alone use 'mi'.

Except for the local buses in Positano and Capri, tickets must be bought in advance at a local shop (typically a bar or tobacconist) or a SITA office. You validate the ticket on boarding the bus by offering it into the machine which stamps it and clips a corner. Do not expect the inspector to be sympathetic just because you are a visitor if you do not have a properly validated ticket. Since the tickets do not carry any destination, only a price, always think about buying the ticket for the return journey when getting your outbound tickets. If you are staying somewhere for more than a few days, it pays to keep a stock of tickets of the denominations you commonly use, in case you find yourself wanting to travel from a location where (or at a time when) tickets are unavailable. Typical fares are listed at the end of the bus timetable section, on page 133.

Timetables are displayed in various locations, as described in the 'Getting about' section for each of the local areas (starting on page 34). You may be able to get a free photocopy of the up-to-date timetable at the local tourist office (but not in Amalfi). When reading time-tables: *Giornale* = daily; *Feriale* = Mon-Sat; *Festivo* = Sundays and official holidays.

Trains. Both Naples and Salerno lie on the main west coast line, but trains are too infrequent to be of interest when travelling between the two cities. Better by bus.

Of much greater interest is the 'Circumvesuviana', a local narrow-gauge network. Frequent trains depart from the station alongside the main railway station in the Piazza Garibaldi in Naples to Sorrento (journey time about 1 hour). The trains on this line also stop at Pompei and Ercolano (Herculaneum).

Boats. All-year ferries *(traghetti)*, jet boats and hydrofoils *(aliscafi)* run between Naples, Sorrento and Capri. Summer-only services operate between Salerno, Amalfi, Positano and Capri, with connections to Maiori, Minori and Amalfi. Timetables and fares can be seen at the quayside ticket kiosks, or in local travel agents (where you may have to pay extra commission for your tickets).

How to get to your resort
Stage 1: from the airport to Naples
Independent travellers not having transfers arranged for them need first of all to reach Naples. You are aiming to get either to the Circumvesuviana station for the train to Sorrento, or to its side entrance on Via G Ferraris, if wanting to catch the bus to Salerno. The easiest way to do this is to take the airport bus from a stop just outside the arrivals terminal (tickets on the bus). A noticeboard there shows the timetable. The bus will drop you directly at the Circumvesuviana side entrance, but you may need to tell the driver you want to stop there. An alternative to the airport bus is the yellow No 14 city bus, a bone-shaking half-hourly service directly to Piazza Garibaldi, for the railway stations. Buy your ticket from the tobacconist in the departures terminal.

1 Circumvesuviana station
2 Side entrance to Circumvesuviana
3 SITA stop for Salerno   7 From airport
4 Bar Pietruccio (SITA tickets)   (airport bus) and
5 SITA stop from Salerno   to/from Salerno
6 No 14 bus for airport   8 To airport (No 14)

For your return to the airport take the No 14, from the corner of Piazza Garibaldi furthest from the station.

Stage 2: from Naples to your resort
For **Sorrento** (also **Positano, Praiano** and **Conca**), take the Circumvesuviana railway. If continuing to Positano, Praiano or Conca dei Marini, take the Amalfi SITA bus outside Sorrento station (tickets from the ground level bar). *Note:* There is also a most useful bus service direct from Naples airport to Sorrento (Piazza Tasso) currently running at 09.00, 14.00, 16.30, and 19.00 (tickets on the bus). Return times from Sorrento are: 06.45, 10.30, 15.00 and 16.30. The journey time is about one hour.
If travelling to **Salerno** (for **Amalfi, Ravello, Maiori** and **Minori**) take the SITA bus from the stop opposite the Circumvesuviana side-entrance in Via G Ferraris. This bus runs at least half-hourly on working days; buy tickets at the Bar Pietruccio near the side-entrance. You can distinguish this from other buses by its sign 'Salerno via

autostrada'. Travel to its terminus in Salerno. The Amalfi
bus from there will take you on to Maiori, Minori and
Amalfi itself, from where the Ravello bus departs. Obtain
tickets for this stage from the Salerno SITA office. The return
journey takes the same route, except that the bus from
Salerno will drop you in the Piazza Garibaldi, not far from
the No 14 bus departure point.

Pronunciation guide

Italian pronunciation follows that of English with a
few exceptions. As examples, simple English words are
used below:

Vowels

a   as in bank
e   as set (short) or as the 'a' in way (long)
i   as the 'ea' in leap
o   as in hot (short) or as in go (long)
u   as the 'oo' in fool.

All vowels are pronounced separately so that, for
example, 'aereo' has four syllables.

Consonants

c ⎫ are pronounced soft if followed by the vowel
g ⎬ 'e' or 'i' (respectively, as the 'ch' in church; as
sc ⎭ the 'j' in joke; as the 'sh' in show). If followed
     by another vowel or a consonant, they are
     pronounced hard (as the 'k' in king; as 'g' in
     god; as 'sc' in school).
h   is not pronounced.
z   is pronounced 'dz' or 'tz'.

Stress

The stress usually comes on the next to the last syllable,
e.g. Amalfi. If it comes on the last syllable, the word will
have an accent, as in città. Sometimes the stress is made
on another syllable and for place names in our area the
index shows the stress if not on the next to last syllable.

The inner man

In the main towns of the region you will, of course,
find a wide selection of grocers (alimentari), confec-
tioners (pasticceria), ice cream bars (gelateria), bars and
restaurants. One of the delights of a holiday, especially
if you have bed and breakfast accommodation, is trying
out a new restaurant in the evening. Since the local
population loves to eat out too, there is a fine selection
of restaurants, often in the most unlikely places.

    Out of town, in the villages, you can normally reckon

Nets are suspended from the trees to collect the olives from the groves at harvest time (Walk segment 57). Buy some to enjoy with your picnic.

on finding only a bar, for drinks, snacks and ice cream. They are often closed during the afternoon siesta period. It is my impression that the very best cappuccino is served in the smaller villages — strong coffee, creamy foaming top, with dark bitter chocolate sprinkled to taste.

Your other preoccupation with food will be to get the makings of a picnic together, another delight. You can buy bread rolls and fillings from the *alimentari* and fruit from a fruit and vegetable stall. Bread rolls *(panini)* are ordered by number but priced by weight and, if the shop is sold out, they will cut off as much bread as you need from a larger loaf. Cheese and other products are sold by the *etto* (= 100gm; plural *etti*) or the *chilo* (= kilo, same pronunciation). Ham is sold by the *fetta* (= slice; plural *fette*). The *alimentari* will usually slice the roll and fill it for you, if asked. Shop hours are approximately 08.00-13.00 and 17.00-20.00. Don't forget to get your Sunday picnic the evening before; shops are not open Sunday mornings.

If you want to add a little extra flavour to your lunch, look for the trays and bottles of pickled and marinated vegetables. Olives are another regional speciality. Some pickled aubergine in your roll will make you lick your lips (and wipe your chin). If your Italian is not up to scratch, just point to what you want.

Flora and fauna

The wild flowers are a treat. Not only do they grow alongside the mountain paths, but the well-paved byways between and in villages also provide a constant feast — flowers thrive on the

Valerian brightens this path among lemon groves between Amalfi and Ravello (Excursion 4 and Walk segment 3).

many patches of spare ground and in the crevices of paving and stone walls.

Research for the guide has taken place in all seasons except high summer and in each month the quantity and range of flowers were outstanding. Here is a list of ones we could put a name to: rosemary, white heather, cyclamen, crocus, orchids (incl. bee and monkey), poppy, freesia, cistus, buttercup, spurge, squill, thyme, mint, geranium, various lilies including asphodel, trefoil, broom, garlic, valerian, vetches, honeysuckle.

Cultivated flowers also enliven the scene, growing in window-boxes and gardens. Bougainvillea flowers into December; the scent of jasmine pervades the paths. You will see an array of vegetables and fruit, including many vines. An abiding memory from our May visits is the almost overpowering scent of lemon blossom infusing the air of the terraces. Lemons hang in plump profusion (see photograph page 93) through winter into spring, to be picked well past the time of flowering for the next crop. In winter black nets (as seen at the bottom of the photograph below) are draped over the citrus terraces as a protection against frost and hail.

In contrast to the flora, the region is not so rich in fauna. You will probably meet mules and some herded goats and sheep, while in summer and autumn the paths are alive with butterflies and lizards. If you are out in the

mountains in summer, there is an outside chance of seeing a snake on the path, sunning itself. In all our visits, we have seen only one. Like adders in the UK, they are poisonous but will move away as you approach.

The footpaths — their nature and origin

Given the steep terrain, it is little wonder that many of the footpaths consist of flights of steps. However, what may be surprising is their high standard of construction, for they are much broader than they need to be for today's traffic (which is very little), and mostly they use well-dressed stone. Often, on leaving the alleyways of the town, the path is no less well built as it makes its way through the countryside to the next village than it was in the town, and street lamps often continue.

These street lamps can be useful when route finding. If you are wondering whether a particular path is one of the public ways, then look for street lamps as a sign — though it may seem strange to see a lamp-lit path leading through olive groves! Another sign of the old public ways is the presence of manhole covers. (The word *fognatura* cast into the covers means sewage. The other name often seen, *Cassa per il Mezzogiorno,* is the name of a former state bank, used to channel economic aid to the poor south of Italy; *mezzogiorno* = south.)

Although I have asked many people, no one seems to know for sure anything about the origin of these paths. Nothing is written about them. One view, probably correct, is that since the region has a long and illustrious history of intense economic activity dating back to the

Even today, building materials are sometimes brought up the stepped path from Maiori by horses or mules (Walk segments 41 and 47).

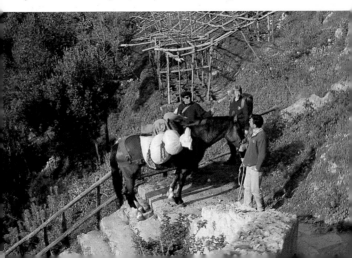

early Middle Ages, a well-founded road network has long been needed. As the terrain is so steep and much of the traffic would have consisted of pack animals, well-made paths were essential. Earthen roads would have become impassable very quickly. Hence the network of tracks paved with stone.

When the motor car burst on the scene, conventional roads were needed. Fortunately, the path network — often consisting as it does of steps — proved unsuitable for modification and so was left alone. Thus the motor roads have been pushed through new ground. This is important to us because, when a path comes up to a road, we can confidently expect the path to cross it and continue on the other side. It is rare to be forced by meeting a road to have to walk along it.

Finally in this section, a word of warning. Marvellous though these paths are for the keen walker, they are held in little regard by the local population. The people responsible for promoting tourism are only now beginning to put value on a wonderful and possibly unique resource. In this age of the internal combustion engine, the paths are little used any more by the local people. A consequence is that, should you ask the way, as like as not you will be directed along the nearest motor road and away from the footpaths. So *be sceptical about route finding advice from the locals,* however charmingly given.

H ints to walkers

The terrain is often extremely steep, so progress is necessarily slow. But the paths are there to be savoured. You find yourself making frequent stops to admire the next view, for photography, or to look into the natural history and villages. Unusual buildings beg to be explored.

For those new to walking. Although the walks described in this guide are for the most part relatively short and follow well-made paths, their steepness may at first seem daunting. Two pieces of advice might prove helpful. First, as all walkers know, the secret of ascending or descending steep paths is to go slowly but to keep going without unnecessary stops. Aim to walk at a pace that allows conversation and smooth breathing. It is all too easy, particularly when going up well built steps, to run out of steam quickly.

Second, when selecting your first walks from your area walk planner, consider taking shorter routes and those with less climbing and an 'easy' grade. Dip into the 'Excursions with picnic section'. Build up to longer itineraries by stages. Also, look for the bus symbol at higher starting points, and let the bus do the climbing.

What to take

Few of the routes pose any problem from a safety aspect. Civilisation in the form of one's hotel or a bar on a bus route can usually be reached within one hour. Where this is not the case, the walk segment description will give suitable warning.

For **weather protection** it will do to carry a waterproof and warm clothing appropriate to the time of the year. The Lattari mountains seem to attract their own weather, and some rain can be expected in any month from October to May. From December to March you can expect a few cold days, with a daytime temperature at sea level as low as 5°C (41°F), while the mountain tops could get a sprinkling of snow (photograph pages 32-33). Outside these months always take protection from the sun in the form of sun hat and long-sleeved blouse or shirt, and be prepared for the occasional thunderstorm.

For **footwear**, the ubiquitous training or other rubber-soled shoe is ideal. As is clear from the relevant descriptions, on just a few of the walks boots are either required or desirable, in which case the lightweight fabric sort are suitable, except in winter.

If you are walking in warm weather, I cannot stress too much the need to **drink enough water** to avoid dehydration. Err on the copious side. I have drunk as much as four litres on a really hot day when doing a fair amount of climbing. The local water supply is safe so, when you have decided on your route, look in the segment descriptions for the tap symbol (➻) to plan your water supply, relying on taps and drinking fountains if possible (take an empty bottle or cup to be able to drink enough when you stop). If you have to carry water, the purchase of a bottle of mineral water on your first day gives a handy container to refill with ordinary tap water on later days. If your bottle has run out and you are passing a house, the request *Per favore, avete acqua da bere?*, showing your bottle, is unlikely to be refused (pair fa**vo**ray, **av**aytay **ak**wa da **bay**ray?).

The walk planners

As indicated previously, the footpaths of the region form an intricate network and, with the help of the walk planner, you will be able to make your way over them at will. The network has been divided into *segments* running between *key junctions*. For each segment there is an overall description of the landscape and a detailed description of the route. If the segment is described in both directions of walking (as is usually the case), an 'a' or 'b' follows the segment number. Below is a section from the Sorrento planner.

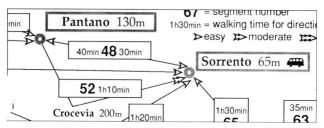

The key junctions are outlined in grey; their height in metres is given; a 🚌 symbol indicates whether they are served by bus (you may wish to take the bus to a high nction and walk down). The arrows show whether a scription is given for both or only one direction, and e number of arrowheads indicates the grade: easy, derate, or strenuous. (For example, Walk segment 52 Pantano to Sorrento via Crocevia is described only e direction, which is moderate; Walk segment 48 een Pantano and Sorrento is described in both directions, both of which are easy.) Walking times for each ction are shown in the box with the segment number om Pantano down to Sorrento allow 30 minutes, from orrento up to Pantano allow 40 minutes).

Using the planner, you can put together any feasible segments to make up varied routes of the desired length, difficulty and interest. For example, you may have decided to walk from Amalfi to Ravello, intending to return by bus. You could take Walk segment 2 from Amalfi to Atrani, followed by Walk segment 3 from Atrani o Ravello, with total (non-stop) walking time shown by he Amalfi/Ravello area Walk planner as being 1h50min. or the return to Amalfi, instead of travelling by bus you ould descend along Walk segments 7 and 6 or 8 and 6. he 'Walk planning tips' for each area suggest some eful combinations of segments.

Grade. This is a measure of the steepness of climbing and the degree to which it is sustained. A segment might rate 'easy' even with quite a lot of climbing if the climbing is spread out into short bursts. It is worth noting that few segments graded 'strenuous' are particularly long and can usually be rendered relatively easy by going slowly and having an occasional rest. Steep descents of more than 200m/660ft have been taken into account, as some people find these hard on the knees and would want to be forewarned.

Walking times are based on my *non-stop* walking times; I walk at an 'average' pace (about 3.5km/2mi per hour). No allowance has been made for major stops. You will need to adjust for your own speed and add in time for picnics and other stops you might make.

The walk segments are divided into six areas, whose limits are defined in the area map between pages 16 and 17. They are: Amalfi/Ravello, Positano/Praiano, Conca dei Marini, Maiori/Minori, Sorrento, and Capri.

Note the following **conventions used in the walk segment descriptions**:

- *Abbreviations; symbol.* CAI: Club Alpino Italiano; AST: Azienda di Soggiorno e Turismo (official tourist office); h: hours; min: minutes; m: metres; ft: feet; km: kilometres; mi: miles; ↦: tap or drinking fountain.
- Sometimes the path will be described as *'contouring'*. This implies progress along a hillside, either level or with gentle rise or fall.
- *Descriptions given in square brackets* [ ] indicate the connecting points of other segments or minor routes.
- To save space, • indicates a new paragraph; ➡ indicates the ongoing route beyond the point where options join.
- Only the *horizontal* distance is quoted. When you are climbing or descending steps, the distance walked will be longer.

Guides and maps

All national and relevant regional **tourist guides** to Italy feature Sorrento and the Amalfi Coast. They are helpful for general orientation and for a description of the major sights. I like *Naples & Campania*, one of the Italian Regional Guides published by A & C Black. Once you have arrived, you can buy one of the many colourful descriptive books, for the pictures and for a run-down of local history. The local tourist offices in the major centres

can supply you with a colour leaflet, a simple town plan and a list of hotels. Apart from in Amalfi and Ravello (where you rely on displayed timetables), they also offer photocopies of up-to-date bus and boat timetables.

As for **maps**, the only one that is generally available is Kompass No 682: Penisola Sorrentina (scale 1:50,000). This does not help with navigating on the footpaths but it shows how the region is laid out and is good for motoring. For walkers there is a much better map, called 'Monti Lattari', produced by the local Club Alpino Italiano at a scale of 1:30,000. It is basically the 1953 national survey, updated with new roads and overprinted with red lines to show the principal CAI routes. The contours and rock markings are accurate, but many of the marked paths have fallen into disuse since 1953. Mule tracks are more reliable. Most of the routes in this book do not follow the red-marked CAI routes, which are mainly for mountain walkers, so you need to be a particularly skilled map reader to get value from this map when out on the footpaths. Still, if you like maps, you will enjoy tracing the routes from the book and looking at the detail of your area, even if you rely mainly on this book for detailed walk directions. The CAI mountain routes are only intermittently waymarked on the ground.

Other useful maps and plans, available locally

The Salerno-based publisher Memo has recently brought out excellent yellow-covered **town plans of Positano, Amalfi-Atrani and Ravello-Scala**, which are widely available locally.

A very precise walking map covering **Massa Lubrense, Sorrento, Sant'Agata** (scale 1:10,000) is available from the bookshop La Capsa on Corso Italia in Sorrento (to the right, as you come out of the Circumvesuviana station). It has historical notes on many of the area's buildings.

The Kompass map of **Capri** (scale 1:7,500) shows paths, some of them imaginary! There is also an excellent walking guide, including a precise map, good pictures and historical notes, entitled *Capri and Anacapri in 12 Tours*, available from bookshops on the island. The AST in the main square will direct you.

Excursions with picnic

There are dozens of ways of spending some delightful hours exploring small villages and out of the way places with little effort or walking, ideal for those hot or lazy days. Here are some suggestions, all of which also have good picnic spots along the way. (For ideas for picnic food, see 'The inner man' on page 11.) Your choice of excursion might let you start straight from your hotel; if not, *travel by public transport is assumed.* Excursions for motorists are described in the Touring section; some of the car tours visit the same places as described below.

Do not think only of outings from your 'home' resort, as bus or boat could easily take you to others.

Excursions from AMALFI

Excursion 1. Spend a couple of hours exploring the tortuous alleys and small piazzas of **Amalfi**. To start with, take Walk segment 1a (photograph pages 24-25), returning along the waterfront (**30min**). Along the way there will be numerous chances to stop for a drink or a meal. A good place to picnic would be at the end of the central pier, sitting on a bench looking back to the town with its mountainous backdrop (photograph pages 34-35).

Excursion 2. Stroll to **Atrani** (Walk segment 2a; **20min**; photograph opposite). Explore its alleys and admire its buildings, often more elegant than those in Amalfi. (Atrani is included in the Memo plan of Amalfi.) Picnic by the beach, in the main piazza or, best of all, on the steps of Santa Maria Maddalena (see cover photograph and the start of Walk segment 3a). Follow Walk segment 2b back to Amalfi (**20min**).

Excursion 3. Take the bus from Amalfi up to the hillside village of **Pogerola**, visit a bar or restaurant (some have super views over the Valley of the Mills shown on page 47), picnic in the small hilltop park near the village centre, look around the old northern part of Pogerola, and then perhaps take Walk segment 4b (**45min**) back down to Amalfi.

Excursion 4. This is a superb all-day excursion which can be taken in easy stages. Although you do have to walk, it goes mostly downhill, can be taken slowly and will absorb your attention with the constantly-changing views. If you are based some way along the coast and can afford only one day in this area, then this excursion is just about the best way of 'doing' **Amalfi and Ravello**.

Take the bus from Amalfi to Ravello. Visit the cathedral and the cathedral museum. Then walk to Villa Cimbrone (**15min**; photograph page 1). Visit the stunning viewpoint, and look round its wonderfully-sited gardens, with many hidden corners and statuary. It's a lovely place to picnic. A bar operates in summer; there are also restaurants nearby.

Now follow Walk segment 3b from the 'Cimbrone Arch' (see ② at the bottom of page 42): walk down past the house and descend to Atrani (photograph pages 12-13; **1h**). There is a good picnic spot on the way, on a level stretch after leaving the foot of the Cimbrone cliff. If you have time, explore Atrani's piazza (photograph page 8 and below) and beach, perhaps taking a drink in a bar here, before following Walk segment 2b back to Amalfi (**20min**).

Excursion 5. Take the Agerola bus to **San Lazzaro**; the journey itself provides sensational views of the coast as the bus climbs in many hairpins. From the bus terminus walk down the main street for 100m/yds, turn left and, after another 200m/yds, turn right on a track. Follow this for 600m (0.35mi) to its end — a superb viewpoint high above the Amalfi Coast. On returning to San Lazzaro, it's worth exploring the village. (**30min**).

On leaving Amalfi, you round a corner and see Atrani nestling under the cliffs (Excursion 2, Walk segment 2).

Excursions from RAVELLO

Excursion 6. In **Ravello** there are two centrally-located picnic spots. From the main square take the broad stepped alley to the left of the cathedral. In 100m/yds, at its top, turn left (Via Toro). The first picnic place is in a small park on the left. The second lies 100m further along, on the right — the *Belvedere Principessa Margherita*, with a stunning view down to the coast (**10min**).

Excursion 7. For a splendid quiet stroll in **Ravello**, with 5-star views and much of interest, see the 'Walk planning tip' at the start of Walk segment 3. This will lead you to a path under the cliff on which the Villa Cimbrone is situated and then back to the alleys of Ravello. It is a walk of about **40min**, but you will take longer, lingering in many places. You could visit the Villa Cimbrone (see Excursion 4 above) or picnic en route. Photograph pages 42-43.

Excursion 8. The path from Ravello down to **Minori** (see Walk segment 5a) makes an easy, pleasant stroll and takes about **1h**. You pass through Torello, one of the few villages in the region without a road, and the mountains provide a wonderful backdrop. Once in Minori, you could visit the Roman villa and picnic in the shade of the Piazza Cantilena, finishing with an ice-cream at de Riso's *gelateria*. If you need to return to Ravello, you take buses via Amalfi (or by alighting at the junction of the Ravello road east of Atrani).

Excursion from MINORI or MAIORI

Excursion 9. Follow Walk segment 39 from Minori to Maiori, or vice versa (**1h** either way). Halfway along, you could picnic overlooking the sea in the fine little piazza by the church of **San Michele** (photograph page 87). In Minori the best place to picnic is in the shady Piazza Cantilena near the eastern end of the sea-front.

Excursion at CONCA DEI MARINI

Excursion 10. Take the bus to **Conca dei Marini** (alight at the Hotel Belvedere bus stop). From here you follow the start of Walk segment 37b, to two superb viewpoints, looking either way along the coast; you might like to picnic at one of them. (The view east along the coast is shown on page 81.) You can visit the church of San Pancrazio, which lies between the viewpoints. Return to the hotel and then follow Walk segment 38 to the beach and bar/restaurants at Piaggia di Conca. Total walking time is about **50min**.

Excursions from POSITANO

Excursion 11. From Positano take the bus up to **Monte Pertuso** (photograph page 32). Look around the village, picnic in the church piazza or visit a bar or restaurant, and then perhaps take Walk segment 19b (photograph page 63) to stroll back to Positano (**1h**).

Excursion 12. From Positano take the Monte Pertuso bus up beyond the village to its terminus. From here stroll up to **Nocelle** (Walk segment 20a; **45min**). Walk through the village (bar/restaurant) and down to its finely-situated church piazza, a shady picnic spot. From here return to Monte Pertuso (Walk segment 20b; **30min**) or descend to Positano (Walk segment 21a; **1h30min**) — steps take you down a wild mountainside with views along the coast and down over the Positano. At one time these steps were Nocelle's only link with civilisation.

Excursions from SORRENTO

Excursion 13. From Sorrento, take the bus up to **Termini** (photograph page 9). Follow Walk segment 53a for **5min**, to the super picnic spot shown on pages 26-27 — a grassy mound with distant all-round views. Return to Termini and then descend to **Nerano** (Walk segment 58a; **25min**) and to the fine beach at **Marina di Cantone** (Walk segment 62a; **25min**; photograph page 115). The bars and restaurants here are open all year round. Perhaps wander round the headland to Recommone and back (Walk segment 62; **30min**). Return by bus from Marina di Cantone.

Excursion 14. From Sorrento, take the Massa Lubrense bus to **Capo**. Follow Walk segment 50 down to the Roman **Villa di Pollio** and picnic with a fine view of the Bay of Naples. **1h** round trip from Capo.

Excursion 15. From Sorrento, take the Circumvesuviana train to Castellamare di Stabia station, to connect with the cable car to the 1131m/3700ft-high summit of **Monte Faito**.

Excursions on CAPRI

Excursion 16. Both the **Villa Jovis** (Walk segment 68; **1h15min** round trip) and the **Arco Naturale** (Walk segment 69; **50min** round trip) offer good picnic spots. On the way you will enjoy good views of the island from Capri's jasmine scented alleys. Bar/restaurants are en route in both segments. Photographs pages 122, 126.

Excursion 17. Take the bus to **Anacapri**. Look around this delightful small town and then take the chair-lift (summer only) up to the summit of **Monte Solaro**, the setting shown below.

Excursion 17: Picnic here at the summit of Monte Solaro, from where there is a superb panorama of Capri and the Bay of Naples. The wild flower meadows just below the summit are exquisite. These three offshore rocks are called the Faraglione islets.

 Touring

If you have not yet decided about taking your own car or hiring one, *do* give some thought to motoring in the region. Parking in the towns is very difficult and the driving is hectic: most roads are full of bends ... fitting perhaps in the country that invented spaghetti. Remember that public buses offer a cheap and efficient alternative means of transport — while at the same time letting you enjoy the scenery as you go.

If, however, you *have* decided to motor in the region, the seven short tours described on the following pages will take you to some out-of-the-way places, fine picnic spots and splendid viewpoints. You will probably also use the car to visit some famous sites outside the area covered by this book — Pompei or Paestum for example — but it is assumed that you will use a road map or atlas to get there; no touring notes are included in this book.

The 'backbone' route of our region is the main road east out of Sorrento: this connects with the SS (Strada

Viewed from one of Amalfi's piers, we see how buildings, topped by the chapel of San Biagio, cling to the cliffs, high above the coast road. Walk segment 1 follows the balcony path beside them.

Statale) 163, which goes south to the coast and then east all the way to Salerno — the world famous Amalfi Drive. This coast road, not described in detail here because it is so well signposted, is a dramatic 45km-long corniche, passing through Positano, Vèttica Maggiore, Praiano, Conca dei Marini, Amalfi, Atrani, Minori and Maiori, before heading east to Vietri sul Mare and Salerno.

The first two tours comprise circuits easily accessible from Sorrento. The other tours consist of mostly short excursions starting from various points along the coast road. See the fold-out area map between pages 16-17.

The best map for touring the area is the Kompass map No 682, Penisola Sorrentina. All the yellow and the wide white roads shown on this map can be driven, plus some of the narrow white roads.

The following motoring hints apply particularly to the coast road:

- In hold-ups, be sure to come to a halt well to the right, leaving maximum space for a coach to get past and leaving some space behind the car in front
- Be aware of the practice of SITA bus drivers to slow down when the road ahead is clear, to let cars overtake.
- Where there is no official parking area, you may have to park in a sensible spot on a road some way out of town and walk in.

Tour 1: CIRCUIT FROM SORRENTO

This tour is only 37km/23mi long, but there is so much to enjoy you may wish to split it into two days. The tour describes a circuit from Sorrento. Various side-trips are included, to take you to the most interesting locations in the area — where you can perhaps walk or picnic.

Suggestions for stretching your legs: Walk segments 53a, 57 (Walk segment 62 is accessible on a detour to Marina di Cantone)

Leave Sorrento by heading west, and follow signs to **Massa Lubrense** (6km ✝ ▲ ✕ 📷). It's worth looking around this elegant old town. Back in your car, continue up the wide main street and go left behind the triangle at the top. Follow the road for 1.4km more to a sharp left bend. Here fork right (signposted to Termini) into and through the village of **Santa Maria** (7km ✝).

Just 0.4km beyond Santa Maria turn right to enter the little village of **Annunziata** (8km ✝ ▮ 📷). Park and explore on foot (see notes in Walk segment 57 and photograph on page 112). Then return to the road, turn right, and continue downhill. After crossing a bridge, turn left onto a more major road. Drive up through **Termini** to the top end of the village, by the church (12km ✝ ✕ ▲ 📷). The notes for Walk segment 53a would take you to the picnic spot shown below.

Leave Termini with the church on your left, immediately turn right at the T-junction, and drive ahead up the hillside, zigzagging to the summit ridge. Park and walk left to the hilltop church of **San Costanzo** (✝ 📷), to see the whole peninsula laid out before you. Continue by car or on foot west along the road to its end, for a superb view of Capri out in the glittering sea.

Drive back to Termini and continue out of the village, leaving the church on your left. *Possible detour:* In just 0.4km you could turn right down to Nerano and Marina di Cantone (♟✕) with its fine beach. See the notes in Walk segment 62 and photograph page 115. The main tour continues to **Sant'Agata** (20km ♟✕▲). From the central T-junction, with the Hotel delle Palme on your left, drive towards the large old church and past it for 0.5km to the gates of **Deserto Convent** (♟📷). Park here and walk up the drive. See the notes at the start of Walk segment 55, to reach the beautiful belvedere here. The old church passed on the way up is worth a visit for its wonderful inlaid marble altars.

Now with the Hotel delle Palme behind you, drive away and after 0.5km turn right at a T-junction with a main road. After 1.6km, at a right hand bend, turn right (signposted 'Eliporto Pineta'). Take the first left (after 0.5km) by a restaurant (✕) and continue for 1km more, to the end of a pine wood on your left. Here at **Capo di Mondo** (📷) the panorama is magnificent, a fine place to enjoy a picnic. Return the way you came and turn right at the main road.

Descend to the next village, **Fontanelle** (28km, car park on the left). From the car park, walk for about 500m/yds to the right along a narrow road (Via Rocca) that starts level and then climbs gently to reveal ever more dramatic views of Vesuvius and the Bay of Naples. Return the same way to your car. Drive out of the car park, turn right on the main road, retrace your incoming route for 100m, and then turn left downhill on a narrow road (Via Belvedere). After about 1km you reach a small car park with a fine view (📷) along the coast to Positano and the highest mountains of the peninsula beyond it.

Return to Fontanelle car park and turn left (east) on the main road to drive in 2km to a crossroads (31km). Turn left and follow signs to Sorrento (37km).

The grassy mound at the end of this track near Termini offers far-reaching views; it's a lovely picnic spot (Tour 1, Excursion 13, Walk segment 53). Capri lies off the shore.

Tour 2: SANTA MARIA DEL CASTELLO AND MONTE FAITO

This circuit (60km/37mi) takes quiet but good roads full of hairpin bends to climb into the mountainous spine of the peninsula. En route is the superb picnic spot shown below, with a fantastic view down to the coastline by Positano. Do not choose this tour if the cloud is low.

Suggestion for stretching your legs: Walk segment 23

From Sorrento take the main road east, signposted to Napoli. Just beyond **Meta** (6km) you leave the towns and start to climb, with the sea on your left. Having rounded the headland and started to descend, after 1km (at the apex of a hairpin bend to the left) turn right into a side road signposted to Monte Faito. Climbing now, pass through **Fornacella** (10km), **Arola** (13km 📷; stop here for fine views down to the Sorrento plain), and **Preazzano** (14km).

Some 4km further on, take the first right turn signposted to **Santa Maria del Castello**. The road climbs in bends up to this church on a promontory (19km ✝📷), from where there is a wonderful all-round view. To picnic in the setting shown below, park at the end of a low wall beyond the church. From here a path leads through a meadow; after 100m/yds it turns right, then left, to the viewpoint. You might also like to walk from the church to the Caserma (barracks) Forestale and back (Walk segment 23).

Return by car down to the main valley road (21km) and turn right to **Moiano** (22km). Here turn right to climb the road up to summit of **Monte Faito** (29km; 1131m/3700ft 📷) and on to the higher summit of **San Michele** (32km; 1278m/4200ft ✝📷). The road ends here; return the same way to Moiano (42km) and here turn right to descend to **Vico Equense** (50km). Now follow signposting back to Sorrento (60km).

From the promontory church of Santa Maria del Castello you can quickly walk to this superb picnic spot, high above Positano (Tour 2).

28

Tour 3: MONTE PERTUSO AND NOCELLE

A 6km round trip from the coast at Positano; see town plan page 59
Suggestion for stretching your legs: Walk segment 20

Leave the coast road near the western end of Positano on a narrow road signposted to **Monte Pertuso** (🚶📷). This lovely little village (2km), with a well-sited church, bar and restaurants is shown on page 32. You can drive further up the road as far as its current state of construction allows and continue on foot to the equally pleasant village of **Nocelle** (🚶📷; Walk segment 20), always with the most stunning of views.

Return the same way.

CHIMING CLOCKS

An attractive feature of the towns and villages, particularly on the Amalfi Coast, is the timekeeping provided by one of the local churches in each place. The time is rung out day and night at quarter-hour intervals and can be read by listening to the chimes of the two bells, which follow a code. No doubt you will want to work out the code for yourself, but, if you are still puzzled: one bell chimes the clock hour; another, with a different tone, the quarter-hour (one chime = quarter; two = half, etc; the full hour might get four chimes or be silent). Usually the hour chime comes before the quarter-hour chime, but in a few churches it chimes the other way round.

Tour 4: THE AGEROLA PLAIN

This 46km/29mi tour on minor zigzagging roads crosses the Agerola Plain (600m/1970ft above Amalfi) and affords tremendous views towards the higher mountains and down over the coast.
You can stretch your legs near Il Casino and San Lazzaro; see text.

Leave the coast road 2km west of Amalfi, following signposting for Agerola and Napoli. The road zigzags sensationally uphill for 10km to the first village on the Agerola Plain, **Bomerano** (12km).

Beyond the one-way section, turn right and continue to the next village, **Pianillo** (13.5km 🍴). From here quiet roads take you to superb viewpoints and picnic spots. The first visits a viewpoint down to Positano, the second leads to a view over Amalfi and the interesting village of San Lazzaro.

After passing the fine church in Pianillo follow signposting to Napoli; you are directed left at two points. Just 100m after the second bend, where the main road sweeps to the right in a wide arc, turn left on a minor road and, after 150m, turn right. This road now leaves Pianillo and

---

MAJOR SIGHTS OUTSIDE THE REGION

Pompei and Herculaneum. These two world-famous Roman cities were destroyed by volcanic ash from an eruption of Vesuvius, their remains preserved by the same ash and excavated. To reach them from Sorrento could not be simpler: just take the Circumvesuviana train directly to either site (Herculaneum = Ercolano). From the Amalfi Coast you could go by bus to Sorrento to pick up the train, or take a locally-organised excursion.

Vesuvius. Last erupting in 1944, it has been completely dormant since. A walk around the summit crater on a clear day offers fantastic views. To get there, you just take SITA bus from Ercolano station (tickets on the bus). An all year round bus service operates to the summit car park (see timetables). From here you must climb about 200m/600ft to the rim of the crater (an access fee is payable at the car park).

Paestum. This evocative ancient Greek site (shown opposite), with three well-preserved Doric temples and a fine museum, rises in a pastoral setting near the coast south of Salerno. You can get here easily from Salerno. A number of bus operators combine to provide a half-hourly service from the Piazza Concordia, on the sea-front below the main station (journey time approximately 1h). Ask the driver to drop you at Paestum, as there is no signposted bus stop. To be picked up for the return, just hail the bus on the other side of the road junction where you were dropped off.

---

heads northwest, then south, and finally west, climbing gradually up the lower slopes of the mountains, until it ends 6km from Pianillo, high up above the coast at a place called **Il Casino**. As there is virtually no traffic, you can picnic and walk wherever you like — the views are superb. Then return down the same road to Pianillo.

When you reach the main road again, turn left and continue for another 0.6km, until a road tunnel is visible ahead. Turn right just before the tunnel and follow a high-level minor road above the village of Campora. You enjoy wide views across the plain and to the highest mountains of the peninsula. Just before San Lazzaro, on coming to a T-junction 5km beyond Campora, turn right. Park 200m further on, by the entrance to a track on your left. Follow this for 600m/0.35mi to a superb viewpoint high above the Amalfi coast.

Return to your car and continue down to **San Lazzaro** (30.5km ☘). Then follow the signs back to Bomerano and Amalfi (46km).

The classical Greek site of Paestum, south of Salerno, and (inset) a mosaic of Jonah and the whale on a pulpit in the cathedral at Ravello.

Naples. With all the delights of the countryside at hand and other famous sights to see — perhaps thinking, too, of Naples' fearsome reputation — you might be disinclined to think of spending time there. But if you can fit it in, you will be taken by its vibrant if anarchic street life, crumbling churches and monuments, and, of course, the archaeological museum, an establishment of world importance. With common sense, you and your (minimal) possessions will survive unscathed. Take a lead from one of the guide books referred to on page 17.

Tour 5: POGEROLA

A 9km round trip from Amalfi.
Stretch your legs by exploring the village and its hilltop park.

Head west from Amalfi and, after 2km, take the Agerola road (as in Tour 4). After 1km, at the third hairpin bend, turn right for **Pogerola** (4.5km 📷). There are bars and restaurants in this splendid little village (some of them overlooking the Valley of the Mills, shown on page 47). The hilltop park, where you could picnic, affords panoramic views.

Tour 6: PONTONE

A 7km round trip from Amalfi; may be combined with a visit to Ravello.
Suggestion for stretching your legs: Walk segment 16

Take the coast road east from Amalfi, through Atrani (photograph page 21). After 1km, turn left for Ravello. Follow this road for 2km; then, just after a hairpin bend to the right, turn left on a side-road signposted to **Pontone** (🍴📷). Park after just under 1km, *before* the village. Walk up to the little piazza, with its bar and view down to Amalfi; you could picnic here. *Do* consider doing Walk segment 16 — it's spectacular, as you can see in the photographs on pages 56-57.

Below left: Looking towards Monte Pertuso, high above Positano (Tour 3, Excursion 11, Walk segments 19, 20, 22). Below right: Walking along the ridge that leads to the Santa Maria di Tramonti cemetery, a

Tour 7: TRAMONTI

This 31km tour takes you from Ravello to Maiori on roads that ring the Tramonti Plain, with a visit to a hilltop cemetery and a wonderful view across to Vesuvius.

Stretch your legs by walking the ridge shown in the photograph below.

The Tramonti Plain lies north of Maiori, ringed by rugged mountains (see description in Walk segment 43).

From the tunnel under Ravello, go left on the road signposted to Valico Chiunzi, gradually climbing the hillside. Some 7km uphill, watch for the road descending right, signposted 'Pietre/Polvica'.

Follow this road downhill for 2km, to where a wide road goes left. Turn onto this and follow it for 1km, to the village of **Capitignano**. Continue through the village, gradually ascending to a cemetery, **Santa Maria di Tramonti** (12km). Enjoy the views down to the villages of Tramonti and up to the encircling mountains. Then retrace your route back up to the Valico Chiunzi road.

Now turn right; after 2.5km you reach a crossroads at the crest of the main mountain ridge (19km). Park and enjoy the view across to Vesuvius, perhaps from the terrace of the nearby restaurant. From here follow the Maiori road for 12km, to regain the coast road at **Maiori** (31km).

wonderful viewpoint with the Tramonti Plain at your feet and a ring of high rugged mountains (Tour 7; Walk segment 44). Poles like those shown are used all over the region to support vines and lemon trees.

Amalfi/Ravello

In common with most of the Costiera Amalfitana (Amalfi Coast), this area is one of high mountains rising steeply out of the sea, riven by deep gorges. Limestone cliffs abound. The natural vegetation is woodland, giving way to grass on the higher slopes but, where the gradient relents in the lower parts, the hillside is terraced for olives, vines, vegetables and, of course, the famous Amalfi lemons. This region has not suffered the depopulation of lands further north so, for the most part, the terraces are kept in pristine condition. They reach into seemingly impossible places, making you wonder how farmers get to them or carry the produce out.

The area comprises three major valleys, those leading into Amalfi (Valle dei Mulini), into Atrani (Valle del Dragone) and into Minori (Valle del Sambuco). Additionally, a short but perilously steep gorge falls from Pogerola to the sea (Vallone Cieco). Wild rocky promontories separate the valleys; at the top of the most eastern of them rises the town of Ravello. The Lattari mountains form the backdrop to the area and frequently rise to over 1000m/3300ft; the highest peak in the Amalfi/Ravello region is Monte Cerreto, at 1316m/4300ft.

Getting about

Buses. The main SITA bus station is located on the sea-front in Amalfi, with a summary of the timetables posted outside (for full details see the boards inside). Tickets can be bought here. Typical fares are shown in the timetable section, page 133. The principal routes from Amalfi go to Salerno; Positano and Sorrento; Ravello and Scala; Pogerola; Agerola (for Bomerano and San Lazzaro). See timetables on page 128.

Amalfi from the central pier, a good spot for a picnic (Excursion 1). The blue SITA buses can be seen at the station; boats leave from the end of the pier.

Boats. Conventional boats and hydrofoils take you (summer only) to Positano, Capri and (all year) to Salerno. For the mainland destinations, compared with bus travel, fares are higher, but journey times similar or less. To journey by boat to or from Positano before or after your walk certainly adds to the enjoyment of the day.

Tourist sights
Amalfi. The classical Roman and Greek civilisations passed Amalfi by but, come the early Middle Ages, its power had grown mightily. In its heyday as a maritime trading republic it rivalled Venice, Pisa and Genoa. A code of maritime law, the 'Tavola Amalfitana', originated in Amalfi and through the inventor, Flavio Gioia, it gave the western world the magnetic compass.

Today, Amalfi (pop. 6500) plays an unassuming role as regional centre. It takes the tourist onslaught easily in its stride and bustles about its own business in a cheerful open fashion. The town itself has grown over the centuries in a higgledy-piggledy way, with houses piled upon each other, making use of every last square centimetre of space, served by a rabbit-warren of stone-paved alleys.

The major sights are: the cathedral of Sant'Andrea, with its brilliant façade (photograph page 40), Baroque interior, and crypt with a relic of St Andrew; Cloisters of Paradise; armoury; town museum; many old chapels;

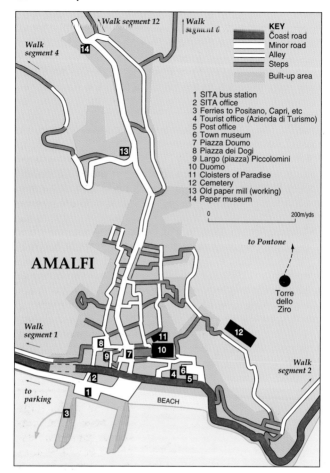

KEY
- Coast road
- Minor road
- Alley
- Steps
- Built-up area

1 SITA bus station
2 SITA office
3 Ferries to Positano, Capri, etc
4 Tourist office (Azienda di Turismo)
5 Post office
6 Town museum
7 Piazza Doumo
8 Piazza dei Dogi
9 Largo (piazza) Piccolomini
10 Duomo
11 Cloisters of Paradise
12 Cemetery
13 Old paper mill (working)
14 Paper museum

working paper mill; cemetery (the colonnaded building that dominates the eastern side of town); small beaches.

Festivals: An Easter procession wends its way from the cathedral through a torch-lit town at 8pm on Good Friday. Every fourth year Amalfi hosts the 'Regatta of the Four Ancient Maritime Republics', a superb spectacle that commemorates Amalfi's former glory. It rotates annually between Amalfi, Pisa, Genoa and Venice.

Ravello. In history, Ravello mirrors Amalfi, as its economic power and influence peaked at about the same time, the Rufolo family being the driving force. The town (pop. 2500) is now quite different from Amalfi in that it is much smaller, being little more than a village, and is spread out

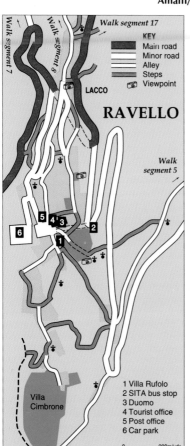

RAVELLO

KEY
- Main road
- Minor road
- Alley
- Steps
- Viewpoint

LACCO

Walk segment 17

Walk segment 8

Walk segment 7

Walk segment 5

Walk segment 3

Villa Cimbrone

1 Villa Rufolo
2 SITA bus stop
3 Duomo
4 Tourist office
5 Post office
6 Car park

0   200m/yds

over its hilltop setting with a multitude of gardens and floral walkways.

The major sights are: the cathedral, with an austere interior, sloping floor and fancifully-large pulpits (photograph page 31); the cathedral museum (downstairs) has a number of relics and some splendid mosaics; old chapels; the villas Rufolo (13th century) and Cimbrone (19th century, in Moorish style) — both have enchanting gardens, laid out in the late 19th century by a Scotsman and an Englishman, respectively. The Villa Cimbrone is a 'must' because of its large and now rather unkempt gardens, resplendent with statues in a spectacular setting. A plaque let into a wall (photograph page 1) records Greta Garbo's stay, when she was rescued by Leopold Stokowski from the clamour of Hollywood to spend times of 'joyful secrecy' at Cimbrone.

Atrani. This small fishing village (photograph page 21) resembles Amalfi's baby sister in situation and character. The analogy may be carried further: blood relations do not always get on well, and there is some rivalry between the two communities. A fruitful hour or two can be spent exploring its delightful piazza, tortuous alleys, elegant old buildings and the dramatically-situated church of Santa Maria Maddalena shown on the cover of the book. Small stony beach; good restaurants and bars.

Walk Planning Tips

A lovely combination from Amalfi which, taken slowly, can fill a delightful day, comprises segments 12a, 16 and 6b. Enjoy your picnic by the Torre dello Ziro. See also Excursions 1 to 5.

Out of area walks: Amalfi has the bus and boat connections to make all the walks in the guide easily reachable for a day's excursion, except some of those around Sorrento. Three outstanding expeditions, starting from Bomerano in Agerola are — *easy grade:* Walk segments 28a and 27a; *some walking experience needed:* Walk segments 28a, 26a, 20b and 19b; *for experts:* Walk segments 30, 23a and 24a. For a stylish way to end the last two walks take the boat from Positano back to Amalfi. Another good starting point is San Lazzaro in Agerola for the segments in the Conca dei Marini area.

WALK SEGMENTS

1 Amalfi — road tunnel (west end)

This is a traffic-free means of reaching the western end of the Amalfi road tunnel, from where three further segments radiate. It is also an enjoyable stroll in its own right. The middle part of the route gives wide views back to the town and down to the sea-front. The path passes the Hotel Cappuccini, a former monastery; its gardens are worth exploring. The route follows a track parallel to the main coast road, initially high above it, later outside the tunnel. **Photograph pages 24-25**

1a Amalfi (Piazza Duomo) to the road tunnel (west end)

Time: 15min; *Grade:* easy, with a *height gain* of 50m/160ft

With your back to the cathedral, go half right across the piazza and under the archway by a jewellers, to enter another piazza (dei Dogi). From the far left-hand corner of this piazza, ascend steps (Salita San Nicola dei Greci). Shortly, turn left up more steps. Continue ascending between and under houses, until the path levels out and fine views open up. Note the buildings set into the cliffside and a minuscule chapel (Santissima Annunziata). Continue to the road at the tunnel entrance. Cross the road and take the path outside the tunnel to its far (western) end. [From here a set of steep steps leads down to the sea-front and breakwater, with good views of Amalfi. Return along the sea-front.]

1b Road tunnel (west end) to Amalfi (Piazza Duomo)

Time: 15min; *Grade:* easy, with a *height gain* of 20m/65ft

Take the path that runs outside the tunnel. On reaching the road again, cross it and take the path that goes up to the right. Follow this path; an obvious line leads to the centre of Amalfi.

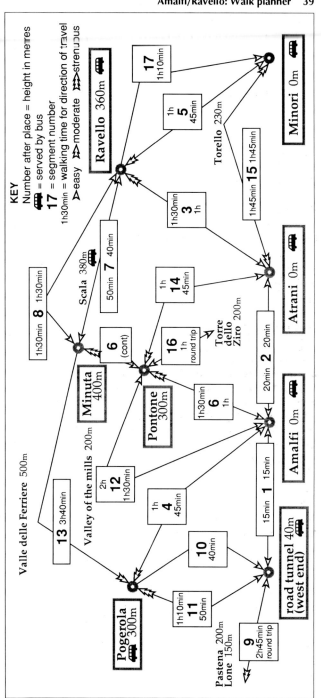

KEY

Number after place = height in metes

🚌 = served by bus

17 = segment number

1h30min = walking time for direction of travel

➤easy ➤➤moderate ➤➤➤strenuous

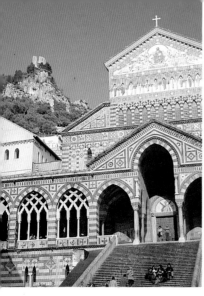

The cathedral ('duomo') of Sant' Andrea in Amalfi, overlooked by the ruined Torre dello Ziru (Walk segment 16; see also photographs pages 56-57).

2 Amalfi — Atrani

A route to Atrani that avoids the busy road and offers a marvellous surprise view of Atrani (when going from Amalfi; photograph page 21). Each end of the route sees the path taking a tortuous track between and under old houses. Photograph page 21

2a Amalfi (Piazza Duomo) to Atrani (Piazza Umberto)
Time: 20min; Grade: easy, with a height gain of 50m/160ft

Take the lesser steps up alongside and to the left of the main cathedral steps. At their top, turn right under the cathedral and then left, along a dark narrow passage. Continue along the winding passage to a small square which opens into a larger square and the coast road. (The town museum is located in the far corner of this square, adjoining the 1st floor administrative offices: medieval costumes, objects and papers to do with Flavio Gioia, inventor of the magnetic compass in Europe; splendid mosaic; the 'Tavola Amalfitana', an ancient code of maritime law.) • On joining the coast road, just past a pedestrian crossing, ascend steps on the left (Salita Roberto Guiscardo). These quickly turn right to run parallel with the road. They ascend between and under houses and, at the top, bend left to reveal a fine view of Atrani. [Steps up to the left here lead to Amalfi cemetery, the colonnaded building that dominates the eastern slopes of the town.] • On reaching the houses of Atrani, take the first narrow passage down to the right (Via Don G Colavolpe). After a few zigzags, just before the steps to the road, turn left up a few steps and then start the final descent to Atrani. At each junction go downhill, until you reach the piazza with its drinking fountain.

2b Atrani (Piazza Umberto) to Amalfi (Piazza Duomo)
Time: 20min; Grade: easy, with a height gain of 50m/160ft

In the Piazza Umberto with its drinking fountain, with your back to the sea, take the narrow dark passageway in the far left corner (by a post box; Supportico Marinella).

Shortly, at a T-junction, turn left. The alley curves right
and then left, rising between houses. Turn right up Via
Torricelli and, shortly, go left at a T-junction. • The path
now leads straight ahead into Amalfi and down to the
coast road at the end of the main sea-front. Turn right into
a small square, then an inner square. Take the passage at
the far left corner, which leads to the Piazza Duomo.

3 Atrani — Ravello

*You climb from Atrani on the coast to Ravello high on its ridge by a
most interesting route. After leaving the alleys of Atrani and its finely-
situated church, the path traverses a cliff high above the coast road.
Later it turns inland and runs among lemon and olive groves along a
ridge, under the towering outlook of the Villa Cimbrone. Wild flowers
(bee orchids and freesias in late March) abound. The views are always
outstanding and rapidly-changing. The path takes a long steep flight of
steps in its middle section. There is a choice of two routes for the final
ascent to Ravello, going left or right to skirt the base of the cliff on which
the Villa Cimbrone outlook stands. The descent is equally fine.* **Photographs pages 8, 12-13, 42-43 and cover**

Walk planning tip: An excellent easy 40min stroll from Ravello's main
square can be made out of the first option in Walk segment 3b, followed
by the last part of Walk segment 3a (see the segment descriptions). This
route descends east from Ravello below the cliff on which Villa Cimbrone stands, re-entering the town from the west.

3a Atrani (Piazza Umberto) to Ravello (Piazza Vescovado)

Time: 1h30min; *Grade:* strenuous, with a *height gain* of 360m/1180ft

In the Piazza Umberto with its drinking fountain, with
your back to the sea, take the far right-hand passage (Via
F M Pansa). Shortly after leaving the passage *either* take
the flight of steps leading up left and follow these ever
upwards to the church Santa Maria Maddalena, *or* continue to the coast road and follow it to the left for 30m/yds,
to reach the broad steps that lead up to the church. • In
Largo Santa Maria Maddalena, with your back to the
church, take the left-hand exit, up steps. Very shortly turn
right (Via Pastina). Climb steps that traverse the cliff-face.
Some houses are reached 300m/yds from church (•• on
right). Take first left, up more steps. • About 40m/yds
along, you come to a house with round windows. [**Walk
segment 15** takes the level path to the right, in front of
this house.] Continue up steps to left of the house, cross
the main Ravello road, and ascend more steps between
walls. The path levels out on a ridge which makes a good
picnic spot. (Now a cliff towers above you, topped by the
belvedere of the Villa Cimbrone; a little to the right a
white house, La Rondinaia, the home of American writer
Gore Vidal, clings to the lip of the cliff; on the next ridge
over the valley you see the village of Pontone and, further

left, the promontory crowned by the Torre dello Ziro.) •
From here ascend more steps, until you reach the base of
the cliff. The path levels out and becomes concreted. At
this point a path goes sharp left. Here you have a choice
of two routes. ① Continue along the concreted path, past
the church of Santa Cosma and houses shown below,
until you reach a minor road. Turn left. After about
200m/yds, look for steps leading up to the left. Take these
to the centre of Ravello. Turn right at the top to reach the
main square. ② Go sharp left. [The 'Walk planning tip'
route goes straight on at this junction.] The path climbs
initially and passes lemon groves for 600m/0.35mi, with
the cliff rising to the right, until it reaches an olive grove.
Take well-made concrete steps leading up right, to reach
Ravello at the entrance to the Villa Cimbrone. Turn left
for the main square some 600m/0.35mi away.

3b Ravello (Piazza Vescovado) to Atrani (Piazza Umberto)

Time: 1h; *Grade:* easy, with a *descent* of 360m/1180ft

Leave the main square towards Hotel Rufolo. Go under
a short tunnel. Now you have two options. ① Turn left
down Via Magruni. This bends right after a few metres
and descends gently to a minor road, where you turn
right. After 200m/yds, at a hairpin bend, take the path to
the right and contour the foot of the cliff, passing the
church of Santa Cosma and houses shown below. When
the concrete surface of the path ends, descend steps to
the left. [The 'Walk planning tip' route goes straight on
at this junction.] ② Follow signs to Villa Cimbrone. After
600m/0.35mi you reach an arch with the name 'Villa

Cimbrone' in ceramic tiles. Turn right down steps on the right-hand side of a house, descending to an olive grove. Turn left along an earthen path, follow it for 600m/ 0.35mi, and come to a concrete path at the foot of the cliff. Turn sharp right down steps here. ➡ Follow the path down the steps, along a short ridge (super views, described in segment 3a above), and then go left down steep steps between walls. Go straight across the main Ravello road and continue downhill. [Shortly, **Walk segment 15** joins from a level path on the left, by a house with round windows.] • In a further 40m/yds turn right at a T-junction. Pass a ↔ and follow the path straight on, down across the cliff-face, to the church of Santa Maria Maddalena perched on a promontory. Take the path from the corner of the square in front of the church, descending between houses to the Piazza Umberto with its drinking fountain.

4 Amalfi — Pogerola

This path provides an attractive route to or from the hilltop village of Pogerola. The easily-graded and exceptionally well-built path is unusual in that it goes through light woodland rather than farmed terraces, with ever-wider views as you gain height. The path wends its way towards the mountains, climbing the northern flank of a side-spur of the main Amalfi valley. Note the quality of design of the steps in the middle part of the walk, which are slightly bowed to left and right to lead rain water to the edges.

Tip: *The 'Cocktail Bar' in Pogerola serves top-class cappuccino coffee and wonderfully-bitter chocolate. There is also another bar and a restaurant with views to the mountains. It's worth exploring the small hilltop park and the old section to the north, with panoramic views.*

4a Amalfi (Piazza Duomo) to Pogerola (main square)

Time: 1h; *Grade:* moderate, with a *height gain* of 300m/980ft

Ascend the main street for 500m/yds, until the road goes through an archway under a block of houses. Then take the side road to the left (Via Casamare). Follow this round the hairpin bend to its end. The path starts here with steps, climbing the hillside and ultimately leading directly to the main square in Pogerola.

4b Pogerola (main square) to Amalfi (Piazza Duomo)

Time: 45min; *Grade:* easy

With your back to the drinking fountain in the

Approaching Ravello you pass under this towering cliff, carved out to accommodate some houses and the church of Santa Cosma (Walk segment 3, Excursion 7). The Villa Cimbrone is set at the top of the cliff.

main square, leave by the alley opposite (by a three-globed street lamp), and turn right immediately, passing the entrance to a restaurant. Follow this path downhill. Turn right in Amalfi down to the Piazza Duomo.

5 Ravello — Minori

This path makes its way at an easy gradient down from the main square in Ravello to the sea-front in Minori, going through the small village of Torello and passing four chapels. It is well built and yields fine views over the surrounding district, with jagged mountains in the distance. The path follows the crest of a minor spur, initially on the landward side and, lower down, on the seaward side. Minori has a wide range of shops, restaurants and bars. The Piazza Cantilena by the basilica near the eastern end of the sea-front is a wonderfully quiet shady spot, maybe for a picnic. Try the top-class ice cream with a wide choice of luscious flavours at de Riso's in the piazza.

5a Ravello (Piazza Vescovado) to Minori (Piazza Umberto)
Time: 45min; *Grade:* easy

From the main square take the wide alley on the left of the entrance to the Villa Rufolo, by a ↦. Go through a tunnel under the Rufolo gardens. Some 200m/yds from the main square you come down to a minor road. Cross this and descend (Via San Pietro) for a further 100m/yds to a chapel with a large antechamber. • Turn left along a level, then gently-descending path (Via Loggetta). After 200m/yds turn right at a T-junction with a ↦. Immediately cross a minor road and enter Torello, reaching its large chapel on the right after 200m/yds. [**Walk segment 15** joins here (Via Toretta Marmorata).] • The path continues to descend gradually for 1km/0.6mi, past another chapel and ↦. Nearing Minori, the end of a road is met, with a cemetery on right. Turn right to pass in front of the cemetery and follow the path to the left, down steps. Just before the last flight of steps to the main coast road (by a defunct ↦), go left under a house and take steps down to Minori, crossing the main coast road.

5b Minori (Piazza Umberto) to Ravello (Piazza Vescovado)
Time: 1h; *Grade:* moderate, with a *height gain* of 360m/1180ft

From the Piazza Umberto, at the western end of the sea-front, take Transversa S Giovanni Mare to a pedestrian crossing. From here ascend Via S Giovanni Mare to the main coast road by a ↦. Cross the road and ascend steps past the main gate of the cemetery. On reaching the end of a road, turn immediately left up the side of the cemetery. Ascend these steps past a further ↦ and a chapel. After 1km/0.6mi you reach the large chapel of Torello on your left. [**Walk segment 15** heads left here (Via Toretta Marmorata).] • Continue ascending between the houses until a minor road is crossed after 200m/yds. Immediately turn left along a path, opposite a **. After 200m/yds, at a chapel, turn half right from the far corner of the ante-chamber. This path ascends to and crosses a minor road to lead directly to the main square in Ravello.

6 Amalfi — Minuta (Scala road hairpin bend), via Pontone

You take steep steps under cliffs and past lemon groves to Pontone and rather less steeply up to Minuta. Views of the Valle dei Mulini open up rapidly and, after Pontone, Ravello comes into view. Both small old villages occupy outstanding sites, with quiet piazzas and ruins of old fortresses and churches. Pontone and Minuta are strategically situated, as other path segments radiate from them. Pontone has a couple of bars. The segment is equally fine in descent.

Walk planning tip: Having reached the hairpin bend (Minuta), if you have an hour and some energy to spare, consider doing just the first part of Walk segment 13 — as far as the fantastic Bosco Grande viewpoint. Return the same way.

6a Amalfi (Piazza Duomo) to Minuta (Scala road hairpin bend)

Time: 1h30min (Amalfi — Pontone 1h; Pontone — Minuta 30min); *Grade:* strenuous, with a *height gain* of 400m/1300ft

Ascend the main street for 400m/yds until you are just past the narrow one-way section controlled by traffic lights. Here turn right up Salita dei Patroni. The path curves left and levels out. Continue parallel with the road until a house stands straight ahead, graced by a mural of the Immaculate Conception. Take the uphill path to the right of this house, leaving the town. The steps go up under cliffs and past a few zigzags to a junction. Now you have a choice of two routes. ① Go straight ahead along a short level stretch and then very steeply uphill past a few houses. After 200m/yds you reach a three-way junction, where each path passes under an arch. [**Walk segment 12** goes left here.] Turn right for Pontone square with its drinking fountain. ② Turn sharp right, to continue rising on steps. [When the path finishes curving to the left after 150m/yds, a narrow steep flight of steps goes up to the right, by a red door; this is a short-cut to the Torre dello Ziro path, **Walk segment 16.**] The main path continues directly up to Pontone square. ➡ Continuing up to Minuta, with your back to the Bar Lucia, *either* turn right up steps beneath the church of San Filippo Neri *or* go straight ahead for about 100m/yds, then take the next right up steps (after a ** on the right), passing the prominent ruin of San Eustachio. • The options converge and lead up to Minuta. On approaching Minuta church from below, do not go straight ahead up narrow steps; instead, turn sharp left to continue on the main path. In Minuta square, go past the drinking fountain on the left and take steps up to reach the motor road at the hairpin bend.

6b Minuta (Scala road hairpin bend) to Amalfi (Piazza Duomo)
Time: 1 h; *Grade:* easy, with a *descent* of 400m/1300ft

From the hairpin bend on the Scala road descend steps directly away from the apex of the bend. These lead to Minuta's square. Continue down to the right, past the drinking fountain. Descending, keep to the main path for 200m/yds, until a fork is reached where the route to the left descends under an arch. Either fork will take you to the square in Pontone, with its drinking fountain. From the square you have two options: ① With your back to Bar Lucia, go straight ahead for about 150m/yds to a three-way junction where each path goes under an arch; turn left here; ② Take steps down to the right of the chapel and to the left of the view point, immediately crossing a minor road. ➠ Both options converge and lead down to Amalfi; the way ahead or down at each junction is obvious.

7 Ravello — Minuta (Scala road hairpin bend), via Scala

This route, largely along the quiet Scala road, is more useful than attractive, as it connects Ravello to other interesting segments, but it does give excellent views of Ravello. Scala's cathedral ('duomo'), with its crypt containing 13th-century wooden sculptures, is worth a visit. There are two bars in Scala; also public toilets and a drinking fountain beside the duomo.

7a Ravello (Piazza Vescovado) to Minuta (Scala road hairpin bend)
Time: 50min; *Grade:* easy, with a *height gain* of 80m/260ft

Take the road opposite the *duomo* out of Ravello's main square, descending gradually and passing the road tunnel entrance. At the first hairpin bend turn right along the Scala road. Some 100m/yds beyond the bridge, take the path to the right; this short-cut eliminates two further hairpins. The path leads to Scala. • From here follow the road for another 700m/0.4mi, to the Minuta hairpin bend.

7b Minuta (Scala road hairpin bend) to Ravello (Piazza Vescovado)
Time: 40min; *Grade:* easy

From Minuta take the road gently downhill for 700m/0.4mi to Scala. Some 200m/yds past Scala's cathedral, by an impressive but defunct drinking fountain, descend steps to the right — a short-cut across two hairpin bends. On reaching the main Ravello road turn left, then go right at the tunnel entrance, up to Ravello's main square.

8 Ravello — Minuta, via Santa Caterina

An alternative to Walk segment 7, this route is preferable, as it involves less road walking. It also makes a foray into wild country by contouring into and out of the head of the valley leading up from Atrani (Valle del

Walk segment 12 takes you past these derelict mills, into a valley of sylvan glades and tumbling streams.

Dragone), passing through a couple of sleepy villages and the outskirts of Ravello on the way. But it is not recommended during heavy rain, as a streambed (usually dry) must be crossed. Cistus and cyclamen will be seen here in May.

Walk planning tip: If you intend to do Walk segment 13, or even just to visit the Bosco Grande viewpoint, take this short cut: in Campidoglio take steps up to the right, just before the first bend left in the road. This path soon turns left and contours for 400m/yds, to the prominent four-way junction in Walk segment 13.

8a Ravello (Piazza Vescovado) to Minuta (Scala road hairpin bend)

Time: 1h30min; *Grade:* easy, with a *height gain* of 70m/230ft

From Ravello's main square, take the broad steps up to the left of the tourist office, itself just to the left of the cathedral. At their top, turn left into Via San Giovanni del Toro. Follow this for 200m/yds, then fork right down an alley (by the Hotel Caruso). After 200m/yds turn right, to reach the end of a road, by a fountain. This is Lacco, the northern satellite of Ravello. • Continue straight ahead between elegant old houses for 150m/yds, where a wide set of steps goes up to the right, behind a chapel. Do *not* take these; instead take the very narrow, level road going straight ahead. Continue to its end (about 700m/0.4mi from the hotel in Lacco). Here it changes into a well-established mule track. Continue along this for a further 600m/0.35mi, until the path forks into two much smaller paths. (Ignore one track going down to the left before the fork is reached.) • Take the left fork, descending to a T-junction with a wider path. Turn left to a stream crossing by a small concrete dam (the streambed is usually dry). The path continues on the other side, gently rising to the left, up well-worn grooves in the rock. When paving comes underfoot (past a small farm), cross a small bridge and climb steps under a chapel (San Paulo). You reach the road by the church of Santa Caterina. • Cross the road and follow the path opposite the church. After about 100m/yds turn right up narrow well-made steps between walls. At a T-junction turn left. Descend steps, then follow a path which generally contours the hillside; at one point the path crosses a track obliquely, by a rustic timber yard. [Shortly after this crossing, very well made steps lead down to Scala.] After about 700m/0.4mi along the path, you come to the road at Campidoglio: to get to it, take a short flight of steps up to the right in front of a chapel, then turn left. Once on the road, follow it gently downhill for 500m/yds to Minuta.

8b Minuta (Scala road hairpin bend) to Ravello (Piazza Vescovado)

Time: 1h30min; Grade: easy, with a height gain of 40m/130ft

From Minuta take the road to the left, climbing gently along the hillside for 500m/yds to Campidoglio. The road sweeps right and then left between houses; where it then steepens, take a rough road obliquely down to the right. In 100m/yds descend a short flight of steps on the right, to a chapel. Here follow a path that contours the hillside for about 700m/0.4mi (at one point, by a rustic timber yard, you will cross a track obliquely). • The path climbs up some stone steps; shortly afterwards, when a house is straight ahead, turn right down narrow steps between walls. Coming to a T-junction, turn left. After 100m/yds you reach a road with a church opposite (Santa Caterina). • Take the path down to the left of the church, passing under a chapel (San Paulo). Then turn right over the first of two bridges, down past a small farm. Cross a streambed (usually dry) by a small concrete dam. Continue straight ahead up the other side and after about 50m/yds turn sharp right uphill. Shortly the path becomes better established and contours the hillside on your left. • Continue along the path; it becomes a very narrow road and eventually reaches a proper road by a small piazza (with a fine view to the east) and an hotel. This is Lacco, the northern satellite of Ravello. Fork left by the fountain and left again immediately, into an alley. Follow this for 200m/yds to the Hotel Caruso, then continue on a narrow road for another 200m/yds, to where you can turn right to Ravello's main square.

9 Pastena/Lone circuit, from the road tunnel (west end)

*Beloved of Longfellow, this hillside to the west of Amalfi, overlooking the sea, is an area of lemon groves and wild flowers. On uniformly good paths, the route visits three finely-situated chapels, including those at Pastena and Lone; they are floodlit and visible at night from Amalfi. The upper part of the circuit has a definite 'mountain' feel about it, and an optional short detour can be made to the edge of cliffs and gorges rising to 350m/1000ft. The segment is described only in an anti-clockwise direction, with the climb (and major points of interest) at the start, followed by an easy descent to Amalfi. **Photograph page 7***

Time: 2h15min (optional detour to Tuoro: add 30min); Grade: moderate, with a *height gain* of 250m/820ft

From the west end of the Amalfi road tunnel, take the narrow road (Via Maestra dei Villaggi) that rises gently between apartments. It shortly turns into a path. Follow this for 200m/yds, until you reach the first of the three chapels on the walk (La Carmine); it forms an arch over the path, with a mural of the Flight into Egypt. [**Walk segment 11** goes up the steps to the right, just before the chapel.] • Continue from the arch for 200m/yds, until you come to a ↦. Here take a path (Salita Pomicara) uphill to the right. The path rises steeply up a gully and then crosses lemon groves for 150m/yds, after which it turns left and levels out. [An earthen path goes right here to connect with segment 11 on its way to/from Pogerola.] • Continue left along the level stretch for 50m/yds, to a bridge. Go left across the bridge and continue for 250m/yds, up to a second chapel with a campanile, at Pastena — a marvellous viewpoint. Continue up the flight of steps from the chapel, cross the Pogerola road and carry on up the hillside to a T-junction with a level path (200m/yds from the chapel). Turn left. • Continue along the foot of the mountains; after 300m/yds, the path descends to a staggered four-way junction in the midst of houses. [Here an optional detour is possible: you can follow the path to the right (Via delle Sorgenti) to its end, to nose into the mountains at a place called Tuoro. The owner of one of the properties on the left of the path might invite you into his garden, to a private but vertiginous viewpoint. Return when the path deteriorates.] • The main circuit continues straight ahead from the staggered junction down an unnamed path (*not* the Via Carammone). On reaching the Pogerola road, cross it and continue down to a third chapel, at Lone, where there is another campanile and fabulous view, as well as a shady plane tree with a seat for a picnic. • From the chapel take steps down to a lower viewpoint with diagonal red-tiled paving. Turn left here: the path leads you straight back to the Amalfi road tunnel after 1km/0.6mi.

10 Pogerola to the Amalfi road tunnel (west end), via Vallone Cieco

This steep and unrelenting path on stone steps makes a dramatic descent from Pogerola to Amalfi. Ascending is not recommended (except for masochists), so only the downward route is described. The path starts descending gently enough between houses, but steepens and winds through olive groves and, finally, a narrow gorge (Vallone Cieco), to reach the coast road at the west end of the tunnel.

Time: 40min; Grade: easy, with a *descent* of 280m/920ft

Take the road from the square beside the church in Pogerola. Just before it ends, descend steps on the right.

Follow these ever downward; as you come into the gorge, they are very steep indeed. The steps lead directly to the west end of the Amalfi road tunnel.

11 Amalfi road tunnel (west end) — Pogerola, via the western rim of Vallone Cieco

This third route to or from Pogerola connects a couple of other paths that could be useful, but are not important enough to merit description as segments in their own right (these are noted in the text below). The path follows the Lone circuit (Walk segment 9) briefly, before striking up to Pogerola, leaving the deep cleft of the Vallone Cieco to the right (on the ascent).

11a Amalfi road tunnel (west end) to Pogerola

Time: 1h10min; *Grade:* strenuous, with a *height gain* of 280m/920ft

From the western end of the Amalfi road tunnel, take the narrow road (Via Maestra dei Villaggi) that rises gently between apartments. It shortly turns into a path. Follow this for 200m/yds, to a chapel that forms an arch over the path. (Notice the mural of the Flight into Egypt.) Take the steps just before the chapel, leading up to the right. • Follow these up some zigzags and then a straight ascent; after 200m/yds, the path bends left and levels out. Here continue to the right, along a level concrete path. [The other path continues to the left. After 50m/yds, steep steps leads up right to the Grand Hotel Excelsior. If, instead of going up these steps, you were to follow the narrow overgrown path ahead (with street lamps!), it would take you through lemon groves to **Walk segment 9**.] • The concrete path contours through woods; after 500m/yds, below the far end of some apartments, descend to the right. Cross a little flat bridge, then continue over level ground for 100m/yds. Some 50m/yds before a house, turn left up steps that ascend steeply to a church seen above. Go round the back of the church to reach the main square.

11b Pogerola to the Amalfi road tunnel (west end)

Time: 50min; *Grade:* easy, with a *descent* of 280m/920ft

Take the steps immediately to the left of the drinking fountain in Pogerola's square, descending to a church. Pass behind this, turn right, and then descend steps by an apartment block. On coming to a T-junction, turn right to a flat bridge, cross it, then climb a few steps. Now turn left on Via Pietralato, which descends gently through woods for 500m/yds. • The path meets another on a bend (see notes in brackets in segment 11a). Turn left downhill. Continue down for 200m/yds, to a large path emerging from an arch under a chapel. Turn left here and follow the path for 200m/yds to the Amalfi road tunnel.

12 Valle dei Mulini (Valley of the Mills)

Amalfi's paper-making industry ('carta bambagina') has been long renowned, relying for water and power on the torrent that rushes from the mountains down the valley behind the town. Sadly, only a couple of mills still operate. This walk goes up past some derelict mills, into a valley of sylvan glades and tumbling streams. It is scarcely credible that this route never extends beyond a mile and a half from the town centre, so remote does it feel. The paths are good, though little used, with excellent stream-side picnic sites, and you can pick your own figs in summer. An attractive continuation to Pontone follows, with super views down to Amalfi from a balcony path. Photograph page 47

12a Amalfi to Pontone

Time: 2h; Grade: easy, with a height gain of 300m/980ft

From the Piazza Duomo, follow the main street up beyond the one-way section, through the arch under the houses and past the Pizzeria al Mulino on the right. In a further 100m/yds, in front of a large building with three arches, turn right up a narrow road. • After only 40m/yds, turn left up a long gentle flight of steps. This path now leads easily in 2km/1.3mi as far as it is possible to go up the Valley of the Mills. On leaving the houses it becomes unpaved, but stone steps are in place for any steep stretches. The path winds through woods, with the stream on the left and passes three derelict mills within the woods. After an overgrown arch is seen on the left, the path rises up a short flight of steep steps. A short level section follows, then another overgrown arch appears to the left, beyond which the path again climbs on steps. Now the path continues for only another 200m/yds, ending where a stream crossing would be needed to go further. • Return to the short level section between the arches, where you will find a prominent path going back sharp right: take this path. After 200m/yds, pass to the left of a small water supply building, then shortly fork left. (This section is a little complicated: remember that you should be ascending gradually, with the hillside on your left.) • Continue contouring gently upwards, initially on an earthen path and later on concrete, passing the occasional house. More houses are reached. At a three-way junction, where each path passes under an arch, go left to the square in Pontone (or head right downhill, following **Walk segment 6b** back to Amalfi).

12b Pontone to Amalfi

Time: 1h30min; Grade: easy

With your back to the Bar Lucia in Pontone square, take the path straight ahead. It ascends a little and then descends. After 200m/yds, at a three way junction where each path passes under an arch, turn right. • Continue along this path past the occasional house, always contouring with the hillside up on your right. Beyond the last house, the path becomes earthen. In its final stretch it passes to the right of a small water supply building and descends gradually to the valley floor, where you meet the path running along the floor of the Valley of the Mills. • First turn right for 200m/yds, to explore the end of the path, then retrace your steps and follow the path past ruined mills and through woods back to Amalfi.

13 Minuta to Pogerola (Valle delle Ferriere)

This well-marked path takes you easily into the rugged hinterland of the Lattari Mountains. Although never more than a couple of miles as the crow flies from Amalfi, up here you are in a different world, amidst high pastures, remote woodlands, and magnificent mountains that rise to over 1200m/3700ft.; superb views abound. After a stiff initial climb, the route contours into the upper reaches of the Valle delle Ferriere and out again to Pogerola, always with the mountain slope up to your right. The path maintains a height roughly half-way between sea-level and the mountaintops. • Those unused to high-mountain walking should note that the path is rough underfoot and that occasionally you need a steadying hand on steeper sections. In a few places the path skirts very high, steep drops; you must be sure-footed and have a head for heights. The path is equal in difficulty to popular high-level routes in the Lake District or Snowdonia. The route is always easy to follow, with good CAI red or red and white paint markings. Because of the views it would be a pity to do the route in low cloud, but no added danger ensues from the visibility becoming poor. You have to cross a stream on stones (not recommended if in spate). • If uncertain of your ability to tackle this route, you could go only as far as the Bosco Grande viewpoint or the stream crossing: at each of these points make a decision — either retrace your steps, or continue in the knowledge that the next part will be just a little more difficult than the last. • If starting in Amalfi, consider taking the bus to Scala and walking up the road from there to the Minuta hairpin bend where the walk starts, eliminating the climb to Minuta.
Photograph opposite

Time: 3h40min; *Grade:* moderate, with a *height gain* of 150m/500ft
From the apex of the Minuta hairpin bend, take the steep flight of steps straight up the hillside. Follow this for about 300m/yds, to a prominent four-way junction. Here turn left along a level path marked with a horizontal red paint bar. [The short cut from Campidoglio comes in here.] • The path contours and rises gently for 400m/yds until, on rounding a bend to the right, what is perhaps the outstanding viewpoint of the whole district is reached. (From this terraced, grassy area, known as Bosco Grande — large wood — there are views down to Amalfi, Atrani, Ravello, and much of the coast. Please close the door on leaving the viewpoint, to keep the mule in.) • The continuing path, now rough underfoot, enters a wood —

The Valle delle Ferriere path (Walk segment 13)

perhaps the 'Bosco Grande' (there is a ↦ here). It goes through a short tunnel and then contours high open mountainside, beside a water pipe, mostly buried, and some signs for a nature reserve. Red, then red and white CAI markings give frequent reassurance that you are on the correct route. • On reaching the main stream, cross at the first obvious spot and follow the CAI marks to the left, along the side of the stream, initially parallel with its downward course. (The stream has scoured interesting rock formations out of its bed at this point) • The path contours the other side of the valley through woods, but for a while with a definite rising tendency. Stunning views keep appearing through the trees, including sight of the valley floor, perhaps 300m/1000ft straight below you. Progress is hampered somewhat by fallen trees. After passing a couple of waterfalls, the tendency is for the path to fall, while still contouring in general. Here you will see large swathes of cyclamen in May and in the autumn. • After perhaps 500m/yds from the second waterfall, the path forks; each fork bears CAI waymarks. Keep to the left (lower) path. It winds through abandoned terraces and then well-tended terraces, improving as it goes. At one point, it descends the bed of a stream which is usually dry. Eventually you enter Pogerola from the north.

14 Atrani — Pontone
This segment provides a useful connection to Pontone. It's a more gentle climb than Walk segment 6, which goes straight up from Amalfi. From a scenic point of view, it is less rewarding than some other segments, but it does give a good view into the Valle del Dragone, which forms a deep ravine in its lower reaches, just behind Atrani.

14a Atrani (Piazza Umberto) to Pontone
Time: 1h; *Grade:* moderate, with a *height gain* of 300m/980ft

From the Piazza Umberto with its drinking fountain, take the road with hoop-patterned paving straight up through Atrani. Just before it ends, by three palm trees on the right, take steep narrow steps up to the right of the restaurant. These bend left, running parallel with the valley floor, and lessen in gradient. Once you have left Atrani, the steps cease, and a gentle incline takes you up to the main Ravello road, 1km/0.6mi from the square in Atrani. • Turn left along the road, go round the hairpin to the right, and then turn left immediately, up a minor road signposted to Pontone. This road carries little traffic and leads pleasantly through a couple of tunnels up to the village. On seeing a chapel on the left, take steps sharp right up to Pontone square. [Or, for **Walk segment 16** to Torre dello Ziro, go left, beside the chapel.]

14b Pontone to Atrani (Piazza Umberto)
Time: 45min; *Grade:* easy

Leave the square in Pontone by the arch to the left of Pontone chapel. Turn right immediately, to the road. Turn left down the road and follow it downhill, through a couple of tunnels, to the main Ravello road. Turn right. Continue down round the next hairpin and immediately fork right on a path. This leads gently down to Atrani.

15 Atrani — Minori
*This excellent segment is made up of three stretches: first, the dramatic ascent from Atrani to Ravello; next, a quiet stretch among lemon groves with fine coastal views; and finally, the descent from Torello on the Ravello to Minori route. **Photographs page 8 and cover***

15a Atrani (Piazza Umberto) to Minori (Piazza Umberto)
Time: 1h45min; *Grade:* moderate, with a *height gain* of 230m/750ft

Take **Walk segment 3a** (page 41) as far as the house with the round windows. • From here follow the level path to the right. When you come to the main Ravello road, cross it diagonally and continue along the path on the far side. It contours past a couple of houses and then becomes earthen and passes through lemon groves. Some 500m/yds from the road, the path comes out onto a poorly-surfaced road that rises to the left. Go left for just 30m/yds, then take the steps that rise steeply to the left. (These steps may be overgrown with weeds at the outset; do not be discouraged.) [The steps down to the right from the road lead into a path that descends gradually to the coast road by the Hotel Marmorata. Just before the road, a steep flight of well-made steps leads to Torello.] • The steep steps

rise for about 150m/yds; then the path bends to the right
to resume contouring the hillside. It runs through lemon
groves, rising gently. After 600m/0.35mi, you reach the
houses of Torello. At the two T-junctions encountered,
turn left. Soon you reach a chapel and the Ravello to
Minori path: turn right and follow **Walk segment 5a** (page
44) from Torello down to Minori.

15b Minori (Piazza Umberto) — Atrani (Piazza Umberto)
Time: 1h45min; *Grade:* moderate, with a *height gain* of 230m/750ft
For the first part of the route you have two options. ① Take
Segment 5b (page 44) from Minori to Torello. From the
chapel in Torello, turn left down the Via Toretta Marmorata. After about 50m/yds, turn right in front of a house,
down Via Vallone Casanova. After a further 100m/yds,
turn right again, to start contouring the hillside. The path
becomes earthen, descending gently. Ignore steps down
to the left. After 600m/0.35mi the path descends steep
steps to the left, and you reach a poorly-surfaced road. ②
To avoid some of the climbing from Minori, on reaching
the coast road by the ⚫⚫ turn left. Walk along the road for
500m/yds, to an ornate building with sculpted heads in
its eaves. Around the next bend take steps up to the right.
After 100m/yds, go right up well-built steps, then turn left.
This path leads up to a poorly surfaced road. ➡ Follow
the road downhill for only 30m/yds, then take the short
flight of steps up to the right and contour the hillside.
Follow this path for 500m/yds, to the main Ravello road.
Cross this diagonally and continue level for 200m/yds, to
a T-junction by a house with round windows. Turn left
here and continue down to Atrani using **Walk segment
3b**, page 43.

16 Pontone to Torre dello Ziro
*This walk should not be missed: it explores the spectacular promontory
that separates Atrani from Amalfi, visits three superb viewpoints, and
culminates in a visit to the castle that dominates both towns, the Torre
dello Ziro. Here the unfortunate Queen Giovanna d'Aragona lived and
was later beheaded. The whole promontory is an enchanting mix of
limestone cliffs, pine woods, rockery plants and wild flowers. The paths
are well built and are probably unique in the district, in that they were
probably built for leisure, unlike the older work-a-day routes. That is,
unless they were built for executioners going about their business...*
Photographs pages 40, 56-57

Time: 1h round trip; *Grade:* easy, with a *height gain* of 100m/330ft
Leave the square in Pontone by the arch to the left of the
chapel. Turn right immediately, down to the road. Cross
diagonally to a chapel. The path goes below the side of
the chapel and descends gently past houses, then it turns

sharply to the left. (Do not be tempted to continue to the left, as this path deteriorates rapidly and ends in lemon terraces.) Go straight ahead along a narrow path at the edge of a terrace. [After about 50m/yds, the short-cut from Amalfi comes down stone steps from the right; see **Walk segment 6a** (Amalfi to Pontone), option ②.] • The concrete steps leading up to the start of the promontory can be seen ahead. Ascend these to a viewpoint, and then descend a little to a level stretch (↔, but possibly defunct). Three paths lead from here along the promontory. The path down to the left leads directly to the Torre dello Ziro along the left flank of the promontory; at one point, about half-way along, you must descend a number of zigzags. The path straight ahead leads to the second viewpoint. • For the best route, go straight ahead from the ↔ up to the second terrace on the right. Follow this round to the right; it takes you to a wonderful broad flight of stone steps, seemingly suspended in space above Amalfi and the Valley of the Mills. Picnicking at the top of these steps, in sun or shade, is idyllic. Here, and at the second viewpoint 100m/yds further on, there are several remains of a medieval defensive position. You can now descend to the path on the left; it leads to the third viewpoint — even more vertiginous than the second, but recently rebuilt in an ugly fashion. Retrace your steps a short way from this third viewpoint, and take the downhill path. It brings you quickly to the Torre dello Ziro path, just above the zigzags. • Return along the same paths — high cliffs bar progress in any other direction!

17 Ravello to Minori

In contrast to Walk segment 5 (the 'tourist' route between the two towns), this segment follows little-used paths, mostly past olive terraces. The views across the valley to San Nicola and the mountains beyond are always magnificent. Halfway down there is a perfect picnic site in front of a small chapel, or, if you are seeking shade, another possibility much lower down in a little piazza in the back streets of Minori.

Time: 1h10m; *Grade:* easy, with a *descent* of 400m/1300ft

Follow **Walk segment 8a** (page 47) from Ravello to Lacco. Continue up the narrow street between elegant old houses for 150m/yds, to a church. Turn right in front of the church, down Via Casa Rossi. Soon cross a road and continue ahead, descending for 200m/yds, to a junction where the level path goes ahead to an electricity pylon. • Do *not* go to the pylon; turn down right, after 100m/yds coming to the Casa Rossa. From this house keep to the left, descending steps or contouring, winding through olive groves. When you come to a T-junction at a splendid viewpoint with Minori laid out before you, turn left and continue downhill. After about 150m/yds, a small chapel on the right, bounded by a low wall and seat, makes a lovely grassy picnic area — though without shade. In late March we saw a bee orchid here. • A succession of steps and level stretches carries you to a slightly rising incline by a green railing. Beyond another level stretch, steps take you down to a T-junction: turn right, keeping to the main path. After another 250m/yds, still descending, now among houses, you come a prominent four-way junction. Turn right on Via Villa Amena, after 200m/yds coming to a shady piazza in front of two chapels, with ✦ and seating. Continue to a motor road; cross half left and go on to enter Minori at a T-junction of alleys. Turn right to pass the Roman villa and reach the sea-front.

Left: Looking down from the third viewpoint to the Torre dello Ziro and Atrani (Walk segment 16). Below: On the walls of the Torre dello Ziro.

Positano/Praiano

Positano lies at the centre of the coastline that stretches from Colli di San Petro in the west, where the Amalfi Drive begins, to the deep cleft of Furore in the east. West of Positano the road runs on a shelf carved out of cliffs that rise sheer from the sea and soar up to the mountains above — a desolate, wild and uninhabited landscape. East of Positano the mountains rise to their highest anywhere on the coast, and hardly less steeply than in the west. But the villages of Monte Pertuso and Nocelle cling high on the hillsides, surrounded by terraces of vines and vegetables and separated by maybe the most profound chasm of them all, 350m/1000ft deep. Further east still the slopes relent a little behind the villages of Vèttica Maggiore and Praiano, to become steep and wild once more before reaching the gorge of Furore.

The paths we use are found only behind and to the east of Positano. Steepness of terrain dictates that this network often consists of long flights of steps or zigzags, but it is well established, mostly not too steep, and beautifully constructed, offering perhaps the most exhilarating walking in the whole coastline — as the photographs in this section testify.

Getting About
Buses. Positano, Vèttica Maggiore and Praiano lie on the SITA route from Amalfi to Sorrento, which keeps to the main coast road all the way. As seen on the town plan, the coast road does not enter the central part of Positano, but keeps behind the town at a height of between 100m and 200m (350-700ft). From the centre of Positano, the easiest means of access to the coast road is to walk up the Via Cristoforo Colombo from the Piazza dei Mulini. (This is the internal bus terminus; buy your SITA tickets in the Bar Mulino Verde here.) Continue up to the coast road to the east of town; this is its lowest point, the Sponda bus stop. The other principal SITA stop, the Bar Internazionale (tickets available here, too), lies to the north — much higher up.

Two local bus services operate in Positano, leaving from the Piazza dei Mulini. A town bus does an anti-clockwise circuit of the town at half-hourly or hourly

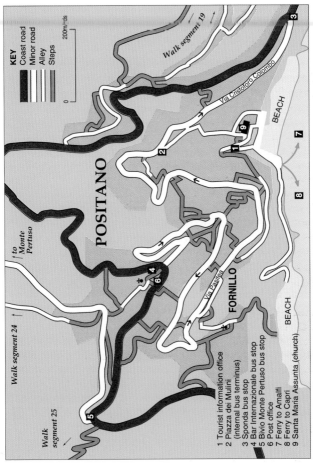

KEY
Coast road
Minor road
Alley
Steps

0   200m/yds

Walk segment 19

Via Cristoforo Colombo

BEACH

POSITANO

to Monte Pertuso

FORNILLO

Via Pasitea

BEACH

Walk segment 24

Walk segment 25

1 Tourist information office
2 Piazza dei Mulini (internal bus terminus)
3 Sponda bus stop
4 Bar Internazionale bus stop
5 Bivio Monte Pertuso bus stop
6 Post office
7 Ferry to Amalfi
8 Ferry to Capri
9 Santa Maria Assunta (church)

intervals. It heads up the Via Cristoforo Colombo to the coast road at Sponda, follows the coast road to the Bar Internazionale, and then returns to the town centre on the one-way town road.

Another bus goes to Monte Pertuso, and continues towards Nocelle as far as the current state of road construction allows (see timetable on page 130). Buy your tickets on board. If you are coming from another town and wish to connect with this bus, you can do so at various stops on the main coast road where it makes way behind and above Positano. Perhaps the obvious one is where the Monte Pertuso road leaves the coast road at the western end of Positano (this bus stop is named 'Bivio Monte Pertuso').

Tourist Sights

Positano itself is the sight, colour-washed houses piled on the curving hillsides, topped by towering mountains. The area behind the Piaggia Grande and along the Via dei Mulini constitutes the centre, with its almost overpowering number of boutiques. Restaurants and bars are to be found in profusion. Around the corner to the west lies a much quieter part of town, Fornillo.

There are three fine churches in the area: Santa Maria Assunta, near the beach in Positano, San Gennaro in Vèttica Maggiore (see caption for the photograph on pages 72-73), and San Luca in Praiano.

Walk Planning Tips

The mountainside behind Positano and Praiano is the steepest of the whole coast. Walking here, usually on well-built paths among pines and cypress, with sensational coastal and mountain views, is utterly exhilarating. But if you're not careful, you will find yourself doing a lot of climbing. Good planning is the key. Use the bus up to Monte Pertuso or (via Amalfi) to Bomerano in Agerola, and start walking from there. A group based in Positano might hire a taxi to Bomerano.

The outstanding circuit in this area starts from Monte Pertuso and requires no walking experience, just some effort: Do Walk segment 22a, followed by 23a and 24a. For easy walks, see Excursions 11 and 12.

From Monte Pertuso, those with a little experience can follow the Sentiero degli Dei (Walk segment 26b), and then take 27a for an easy return by bus from Vèttica to Positano. The Sentiero degli Dei can also be done by those staying in Amalfi: start from Bomerano and do Walk segments 28a, 26a, 20b and 19b.

The best of all the mountain routes is Walk segment 30 (only for experts), which starts from Bomerano.

WALK SEGMENTS

18 Positano circuit

This little circuit of Positano takes you to the quieter parts of Fornillo beach and town, and back through the centre of Positano. You will walk entirely by passageways and steps, meeting motor roads only to cross them. The climb up from Fornillo beach is quite sustained. You could follow the route on the excellent town plan published by Memo or use that plan to do other walks in the town.

Time: 45min; *Grade:* moderate, with a *height gain* of 140m/460ft

From the west end of the main beach (the right-hand end, when you are looking out to sea), take the delightful

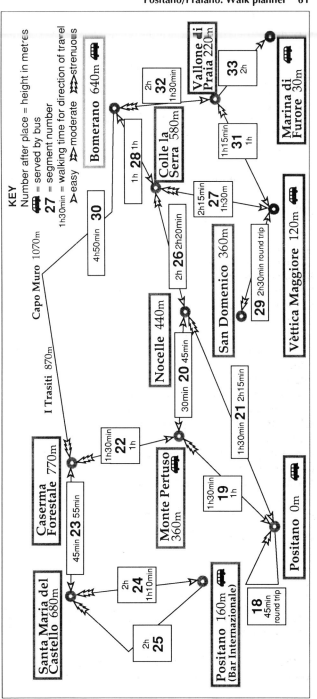

KEY

Number after place = height in metres

🚌 = served by bus

27 = segment number

1h30min = walking time for direction of travel

➤easy ➤➤moderate ➤➤➤strenuous

coastal path (Via d'America) around the headland into a small valley. Ignore the tunnel and continue round to Fornillo beach. Follow paving slabs set in the sand past buildings on the right, to find steps leading up the hill. Ascend these until you reach Fornillo church. • Here keep right along a level path which takes you round to the right, into and out of a valley and up to a T-junction, where you turn right along a level path to a road. Go right along the road and then immediately turn left up steps (Via Martanetti) to another road. Here turn right but, after 40m/yds, turn left along a narrow alley (Via dei Glicini). • On coming to a T-junction by a road, turn right and descend the path. After 100m/yds cross a road and descend (Via San Giovanni) to a tiny piazza in front of a chapel. Turn left or right here; both routes descend to the road again (↦ here). • Cross the road half left and descend (Via degli Oleandri) a few zigzags to a T-junction. Turn left (signposted 'alla spiaggia'), to reach the centre of town again, behind the main beach.

19 Monte Pertuso — Positano

Monte Pertuso is a small quiet village perched in a commanding position on the mountainside 365m/1200ft above Positano. It takes its name from a crag above, pierced ('pertuso') by an enormous hole. The village is important to walkers because the local bus service from Positano gives effortless height gain to the start of some fine walks. In the village you will find a splendidly-situated old church (Santa Maria delle Grazie), a bar, restaurants and an excellent 'alimentari' for your picnic shopping. There are ↦s by the churchyard entrance and 50m/yds to the left of the 'alimentari'. Photographs pages 32, 63

19a Positano to Monte Pertuso
Time: 1h30min; Grade: strenuous, with a height gain of 360m/1180ft

From the main beach at Positano, ascend to the church; beyond it, go left up Via dei Mulini, towards the local bus terminus in the Piazza dei Mulini. About 100m/yds short of the bus terminus, turn sharp right up Via Leucosia; this takes you to a road (Via Cristoforo Colombo). Here turn right up the road. • After 100m/yds, look for steps ascending left. These lead after 150m/yds to the main coast road. Turn left for 20m/yds, then go right up steps by a SITA bus stop (also signposted 'Cimitero'). • These steps lead to a footbridge. Cross it and turn right. Follow the path, always ascending, to Monte Pertuso. At a junction midway up the hillside, keep right.

19b Monte Pertuso to Positano
Time: 1h; Grade: easy, with a descent of 260m/850ft

Two descents are possible. ① From the main piazza on the 'mountain' side of the road in Monte Pertuso, take the

You pass under these cliffs on the descent from Monte Pertuso to Positano if you take the second option in Walk segment 19b.

path straight across the road, to pass to the right-hand side of the church. [You can also reach this path round the back of the church.] • This path winds between houses and descends, keeping left at a couple of junctions, to reach the hillside among terraces. The path descends, mostly through olive groves and down steps, to the upper houses of Positano and later a footbridge over a gully on the left. ② From the piazza follow the road downhill to the right for 250m/yds, to the first right-hand bend. Here go down steps, turning right after just 10m/yds. Broad steps take you down to the first houses in Positano and a T-junction. Turn left and continue for 100m/yds, to reach a footbridge. ➡ Cross the bridge and descend to the main coast road by a SITA stop (for buses to other towns). To reach the centre of Positano, go left for 20m/yds and find steps descending right.

20 Monte Pertuso — Nocelle

*Nocelle lies in a position on the mountainside equally as commanding as that occupied by Monte Pertuso, some 80m/250ft higher and 1km further east. It is separated from Monte Pertuso by a 350m/1000ft-deep chasm. Nocelle consists of just one delightful flower-filled alley contouring the hillside and a path leading down to its church (by a shrine and a ➡). The shrine offers shelter from rain, with seats. You can picnic here or in the piazza by the church. There is also a bar/restaurant with a dramatic view. Among villages in the district Nocelle is very unusual, in that it has no motor road. But at time of writing the road is being extended from Monte Pertuso to Nocelle. **Photograph page 32**

20a Monte Pertuso to Nocelle

Time: 45min; *Grade:* easy, with a *height gain of 60m/200ft*
From the piazza in Monte Pertuso, turn left to ascend the road. Follow this for 1.5km/1mi, to where it crosses the ravine via an impressive arched bridge. *Note:* if you are taking the bus from Positano and you are content to miss Monte Pertuso, stay on the bus to the head of the road at

this bridge. (When the road is finished, the bus will continue to Nocelle.) • Just *before* the bridge, look for a way down to the footbridge spanning the gorge below the road bridge. (When the road is complete, perhaps the path will leave the road just *beyond* the road bridge.) The well-built concrete path heads right from the footbridge, across the steep hillside to Nocelle. Once in Nocelle, you see the restaurant after 50m/yds and the central path junction with the shrine after 150m/yds.

20b Nocelle to Monte Pertuso
Time: 30min; *Grade:* easy

From the central path junction by the shrine in Nocelle, take the level concrete path. This leads out of the village and across a steep hillside, to the road. Follow the road down to Monte Pertuso.

21 Nocelle — Positano

Before the path from Monte Pertuso was built, in comparatively recent times, the main link to civilisation for the inhabitants of Nocelle was an imposing flight of steps directly down the mountainside to the main coast road. It is hardly surprising, therefore, that these steps are remarkably well constructed and easily graded, though they carry hardly any traffic nowadays. For the walker they offer a splendid easy circuit from Positano: take the bus to Monte Pertuso and follow Walk segment 20 to Nocelle; then return to Positano as described below. You have to be a bit of a masochist to ascend from the road to Nocelle, but some people do it just the same, so directions for walking up are given as well — Walk segment 21b.

21a Nocelle to Positano
Time: 1h30min; *Grade:* easy, with a *descent* of 340m/1120ft

From the central path junction by the shrine in Nocelle, take the steps down to the shady piazza in front of the small church, Santa Croce. From here steps lead down past the cemetery and out onto the wild hillside. The steps lead through light woodland redolent of rosemary, with dramatic glimpses of Positano, the coast and the mountainous backdrop. Half-way down there is a small cave containing a statuette of the Madonna, where you could shelter from rain. Near the coast road you pass some houses set in flower gardens. • On reaching the road turn right. [After just a few metres/yards, steps lead down to a public beach.] In the short space of 1km/0.6mi, this road takes you across three valleys, to the fork where Via Cristoforo Colombo leads down to the centre of Positano. At the second left-hand bend, notice the water trough donated by a Lady Banbury and maintained by the Italian League for the Protection of Animals. A ↦ here now provides water for human travellers.

21b Positano to Nocelle
Time: 2h15min; *Grade:* strenuous, with a *height gain* of 420m/1375ft

From the main beach at Positano, ascend to the church; beyond it, go left up Via dei Mulini, towards the local bus terminus in the Piazza dei Mulini. About 100m/yds short of the bus terminus, turn sharp right up Via Leucosia; this takes you to a road (Via Cristoforo Colombo). Here turn

An excellent path leads up high above Monte Pertuso to the Caserma Forestale (Walk segment 22).

right up to the main coast road. Turn right (towards Amalfi) and follow the road for 1km/0.6mi, around three right-hand bends. (At the second bend notice the water trough and ↔; see notes in **Walk segment 21a**). Beyond the third bend, look for steps ascending on the left, by a SITA stop (there is also a telephone kiosk below these steps). • Ascend the steps to Nocelle. See description of this path in **Walk segment 21a**.

22 Monte Pertuso — Caserma Forestale

*The steep mountainside behind Monte Pertuso, clad in the most aromatic of cypresses, pines, rosemary and myrtle, affords outstanding views along the coast and up into the highest of the Lattari Mountains. This segment gives access to a set of well-constructed paths crossing the mountainside. The Caserma (barracks) Forestale is a solid stone building with two grilled windows, nestling in the forest. The path has to gain a fair amount of height — hence the 'strenuous' grade — but it is not too steep and is in shade for much of the way. An optional extension is described to one of the outstanding viewpoints of the peninsula, 'I Trasiti', a superb picnic spot. **Photographs pages 32, 65, 78-79***

22a Monte Pertuso to the Caserma Forestale

Time: 1h30min (for the detour to the Trasiti viewpoint, add 100m/330ft; 35min return); *Grade:* strenuous with a *height gain* of 400m/1300ft

Take the road uphill from Monte Pertuso and go 100m/yds beyond the first right-hand bend, then climb left up steps. (If travelling by bus, alight here, *one stop beyond* Monte Pertuso.) These steps, steep at first but gradually easing into a path as they rise, lead all the way to the Caserma Forestale. Orange and red marks, relics of an old waymarking system, guide you. The path zigzags straight uphill for the first half of the climb and then goes mainly left. *Note: After perhaps an hour's climbing, keep on the level; ignore the steps rising to the right.* • From the Caserma Forestale, you can take a detour to the Trasiti viewpoint. To get there, take the zigzag path behind the Caserma for 100m/yds, then turn right on the lower of two tracks marked with red/white CAI waymarks. This track leads gradually up to the rocky shelf seen in the photograph on pages 78-79, after 20 minutes' walking from the Caserma and 100m/330ft of ascent. In clear weather you can see along the coast as far as Capri, with Ischia off to the right. Below lies the village of Nocelle. To the left, the path emerging from the enormous rocky chasm is the route by which intrepid souls doing **Walk segment 30** reach I Trasiti. Return to the Caserma by the same route. One December we met two men here carrying baskets overflowing with *porcini* mushrooms.

22b Caserma Forestale to Monte Pertuso
Time. 1h; *Grade:* easy, with a *descent* of 400m/1300ft

Take the path going down from the Caserma Forestale, which leads down to the road above Monte Pertuso. The path goes mainly left across the slope in its first half and then zigzags straight down. Turn right on the road.

23 Caserma Forestale — Santa Maria del Castello
Santa Maria del Castello is a church sitting on a promontory high above Positano. There is a restaurant nearby. Connecting the church to the Caserma lies a wonderfully-constructed balcony path that threads its way at an easy gradient between the pines, with the most stunning views down a wild cypress-studded mountainside to Positano. Confusingly, signs have been erected recently to label this as the 'Sentiero degli Dei', the name rightfully given to Walk segment 26. This is a walk to savour.

23a Caserma Forestale to Santa Maria del Castello
Time: 45min; *Grade:* easy

Looking down the hillside at the Caserma Forestale, take the well-built path to the right; initially it rises gently. It is joined shortly by another path and starts a gently-descending traverse across the mountainside lasting 2km/1.2mi. On emerging from the forest, the path threads through some smallholdings, to reach a road. Turn left and walk 400m/yds to the church.

23b Santa Maria del Castello to the Caserma Forestale
Time: 55min; *Grade:* easy, with a *height gain* of 90m/300ft

From the church drive turn right along the road for 400m/yds. Turn right again, on a rough concrete road through some smallholdings. After about 100m/yds, as it enters the forest, this becomes a well-built path, which now traverses the mountainside, gently ascending. After 2km/1.2mi, a prominent fork is reached: go right on the gently descending path for about 100m/yds to the solid stone building of the Caserma Forestale. Now consider making a detour to the Trasiti viewpoint (see **Walk segment 22a**).

24 Santa Maria del Castello — Positano
*This well-graded ancient paved path provides a sensational yet easy return from the heights of Santa Maria del Castello to the fleshpots of Positano. Zigzagging down, you see the roofs of the town and the beach as in an aerial photograph, with extensive panoramas left to the Lattari mountain range. You might consider making the ascent if it's not too hot; I once met a middle-aged woman, obviously a local, climbing slowly in her underclothes, black dress neatly folded over an arm. I scarcely think she expected to meet anyone that evening. Although rated strenuous on account of the height difference, the path is not too steep and has few steps. **Photograph pages 68-69**

24a Santa Maria del Castello to Positano (Bar Internazionale)
Time: 1h10min; *Grade:* easy, with a *descent* of 520m/1700ft

Leaving the church drive, turn left. In 200m/yds you come

to a crossing of minor roads: turn left. The narrow tarmac road turns right after 50m/yds: here continue straight ahead on a field path. Once at the edge of the plateau, go left for 100m/yds, to find the start of the paved path down to Positano. • The path descends a wild mountainside, finally reaching the upper houses of Positano and the Monte Pertuso road. Cross straight over the road and descend to a small piazza by the Chiesa Nuova. Follow the path round the right-hand side of the church to its rear, and descend to the main coast road by the Bar Internazionale (SITA stop and tickets; refreshments).

24b Positano (Bar Internazionale) to Santa Maria del Castello
Time: 2h; *Grade:* strenuous, with a *height gain* of 520m/1700ft

From the Bar Internazionale take the Via Chiesa Nuova; it ascends straight up from the junction at the bend in the coast road. Beyond the church, steps take you up to the Monte Pertuso road. Go straight across, to join the path that climbs the mountainside. About one-third of the way up, ignore a minor path going straight ahead; the main path turns sharp right. • At the top of the path, turn sharp left to contour on a field path just below the rim of the plateau. After only 100m/yds, watch for a path going right and take it. After another 100m/yds, this leads you to a

This ancient paved path snakes down the hillside from Santa Maria del Castello to Positano (Walk segment 24). Besides admiring the panoramic views you will feast your eyes on the orchids, rosemary, broom and many other flowers beside the path. The view on pages 28-29 is taken from further left, just below Santa Maria del Castello.

crossing of minor roads. Turn right and reach the church of Santa Maria in a further 200m/yds.

25 Positano — Santa Maria del Castello

If wishing to ascend from the Bar Internazionale to Santa Maria del Castello on a hot day, you can take this segment as a shady alternative to the full sun of Walk segment 24. After a steep start it is generally less steep, too. It takes a now little-used but excellently-built path on the forest-clad slopes to the northwest of Positano. (In its upper reaches, the path becomes rougher, and it is preferable to wear walking boots .) As you gain height, first glimpses and then full views of the coast and mountains are revealed. In May you will see many orchids. Only the ascent is described, as Walk segment 24, with its tremendous views, offers the obvious way down.

Time: 2h; *Grade*: strenuous, with a *height gain* of 530m/1740ft

From the Bar Internazionale walk west along the coast road for 300m/yds, to the Monte Pertuso turn-off. After just 30m/yds more, take the steep flight of steps, currently signposted 'Itinerario 1'. These zigzag, but soon the gradient relents, and an excellent path ascends the left-hand side of the valley, into the mountains. On coming to an isolated house (**25min**), pass to the left of it, to regain your stepped path. Before long this makes three zigzags and then heads left. At about **45min** take a prominent turning sharp right (currently signposted 'per S Maria'), ignoring

Vineyards cling to the hillsides below the 'path of the Gods' (Sentiero degli Dei; Walk segment 26).

the smaller path going straight ahead. For a short while there are red paint waymarks. • From here the path will climb steadily to the summit, always with the slope up to the left (apart from some minor zigzags). Some 500m/yds along this path (**1h15min**), ignore the broad level path heading right; fork left, to ascend. After another 100m/yds (**1h22min**), at another fork, ignore the path on the left (alongside a barbed-wire fence); keep right on the lower, smaller path (a small stretch of which is in poor condition). On reaching easier grassy slopes, the path turns inland and joins the end of a narrow road. Turn right here, pass a house, and then go left around the bend, to a minor cross-roads. Turn right and continue for 200m/yds to Santa Maria del Castello.

26 Colle la Serra — Nocelle

*The wild mountainside east of Nocelle can be traversed along a well-waymarked but rough path that offers magnificent views of the mountains and coast, and lives up to its billing as the 'path of the Gods' (Sentiero degli Dei). Typically this segment will form part of a route from Bomerano to Positano (for walkers coming from Amalfi), or from Monte Pertuso to Vèttica Maggiore (for those starting in Positano). • This route should be undertaken only by confident walkers as, once committed, there are no escape routes, and you must rely on waymarks to show the route. The red dot waymarks are frequent so, if you have not seen one for about 50m/yds, retrace steps! Be especially alert when the path winds between bushes. Long trousers and boots are most people's preferred kit for this walk. Take enough water, too, as bottles may be replenished only at each end of the segment. **Photograph above***

26a Colle la Serra to Nocelle
Time: 2h; *Grade:* easy

At the Colle la Serra, with your back to the white house

with a crucifix, pick up the orange/red dot waymarks, following the narrow path that ascends straight ahead. Then it bends up left, away from an abandoned building. The path soon levels off among terraces. The waymarks are your guide for the next two hours, as you make way across the wild mountainside, either on the level or with a gently descending tendency, and always with the slope up to your right. Any ascents will be short-lived. • You enter Nocelle on a level path by houses. This turns sharp left down a few steps, to a path junction in the centre of the village, where you will find a shrine and ➡

26b Nocelle to Colle la Serra
Time: 2h20min; *Grade:* moderate, with a *height gain* of 140m/460ft
From the path junction by the shrine in the centre of Nocelle, climb the steps, soon turning right and heading out of the village. Look for the first red/orange dot waymarks. These are your guide for the next two hours, as you make way across the wild mountainside, either on the level or with a gently ascending tendency, and always with the slope up to your left. Any descents will be short-lived. • As you near the col (la Serra), you will see a few terraces and the path will lead you past an abandoned building, to a junction of wide mule tracks, near a white house with a crucifix on its garden wall.

27 Colle la Serra — Vèttica Maggiore (or Praiano)
*Rough-hewn but solid steps and terraces lead from the col down to the coast towns, traversing a lonely, wild, beautiful hillside that was once quite intensively cultivated. Views west extend to Positano and the coast as far as Capri, while in the middle of the walk you get a good view of the monastery of San Domenico (Walk segment 29). • At the lower end of the path proper, but still some way above the towns, there is an outstanding viewpoint from where, on a clear day, you would be able to look along the whole coastline from Capri to Salerno. This could form the objective of a shortish walk for someone staying in one of the two towns — take the first part of Walk segment 27b. See notes on Vèttica in the caption for the **photograph on pages 72-73**.*

27a Colle la Serra to Vèttica Maggiore (and Praiano)
Time: 1h30min; *Grade:* easy, with a *descent* of 400m/1300ft
From the junction of mule tracks at the Colle la Serra, walk to the right of the crucifix on the garden wall of the white house. Descend steps for 100m/yds to a T-junction; here turn left. At a junction (with ➡) 300m/yds further on, go straight ahead. Continue to descend steps, always with the slope up to the left. At times the path follows the edges of terraces. After about 1km/0.6mi, the path passes a water supply building and then rounds the crest of the ridge, turning to the left. This is a splendid viewpoint.

• Some 150m/yds further on, now on the eastern side of the ridge, turn right down a steep flight of steps (passing through an arch in a house), down to a road. [If you wish to continue on **Walk segment 31a** to Furore from here, go left to the end of the road; then refer to the segment description on page 77.] • Cross the road and descend more steps, to a horizontal alley [where **Walk segment 31b** comes in from the left]. Those based at Praiano may wish to descend further, along Via Oratorio, and then turn right lower down, to reach Praiano's large church. To continue to Vèttica, turn right along the horizontal alley. After 300m/yds you come to a superb viewpoint in front of a small chapel. • Just beyond the chapel, descend the concrete steps and turn left at the bottom, down to a road. Cross this and descend eight more steps, to a lower road; turn right. This road narrows into an alley, descending gently between houses. After 200m/yds along the alley, you can turn left opposite a ↔, down to the main coast road near the centre of Vèttica. Or take the next left, for a more pleasant, if slightly longer, way down.

27b Vèttica Maggiore (or Praiano) to Colle la Serra
Time: 2h15min; *Grade:* strenuous, with a *height gain* of 460m/1500ft
Starting from the main coast road just above Vèttica church, in the small piazza (G Gagliano) with a fountain, climb the steps (Via F Russo). After 40m/yds turn left into an alley that takes you by easy stages up to a T-junction

with a horizontal alley. Turn right here, soon passing a
↦. • This alley rises gently between houses for 200m/yds
and then breaks out onto an unsurfaced road. Just before
joining another road, take the eight steps up to the left.
Cross the road and climb more steps, soon turning right
and ascending to a small chapel — from where there is
a splendid view. • Now follow the motor road that
ascends from the chapel until it levels out and starts to
descend. Here take steps going steeply up to the left,
passing through an arch under a house. [Those based in
Praiano can reach this point from their large church by
taking the alley that goes between the church and the
campanile. Turn left behind the church, to ascend steeply
to the road, crossing a horizontal alley en route.] •
Continue straight up beyond the house with the arch, until
the path turns left. In a further 150m/yds, where the path
moves over to the west side of the ridge, you will reach
the splendid viewpoint mentioned in the introduction to
this segment. • The path now ascends on steps, inter-
spersed with level stretches along the edges of terraces.
The hillside is always on your right. At a couple of
junctions near the top of the climb (↦ at one of them),
keep ahead up steps. You will know that you have
reached the Colle la Serra: there is a junction of wide
mule tracks here, by a crucifix on the garden wall of a
white house.

*Looking west across Vèttica Maggiore
to Positano and the coastline as far as
Capri (Walk segments 27, 29, 31).
The domes of the church of San Gennaro
glisten in early morning sunlight.
This church, and its wide piazza just
below the road, are well worth a visit.
The bronze doors consist of fourteen
finely-cast panels depicting San
Gennaro's life story, and nearby there
are bronze busts of Matthew, Mark, Luke
and John. There is a tap in an alley just
below the church and the path to the
beach leads down from here.*

28 Bomerano — Colle la Serra

Easy walking across a steep rugged hillside connects Bomerano with the Sentiero degli Dei which leads to Nocelle (Walk segment 26), or Walk segment 27 down to Vèttica/Praiano. En route you pass under the cave of Grotta Biscotta, which is reputed to contain medieval animal pens. • The Agerola bus from Amalfi takes a most sensational route. The road gains height consistently in a series of bends and tunnels that follow the contours of the terrain, threading through communities clinging to the mountainside. After passing into and out of the deep valley of Furore, the road starts on a series of serpentine bends through the village of Furore, noted for its artists' colony and for fine wine, to arrive finally at the 600m/ 2000ft-high plain of Agerola. Spare a thought for the cyclists of the Tour of Italy, who must sometimes make this climb — at the summit there is a monument to the legendary Italian cyclist Fausto Coppi. • You could alight at the second stop after the bus has finished the climb and driven into the plain; there is a good 'alimentari' at this stop. On leaving the shop, follow the road to the left for 600m/0.35mi, to Bomerano's main square. The third bus stop (half a kilometre after the bus has taken the next two bends, by a no entry sign) is nearer the square: take the narrow road left by the no entry sign. There is no ↦ in Bomerano.

28a Bomerano to Colle la Serra
Time: 1h; *Grade:* easy

Facing the large church in Bomerano, take the narrow road going left out of the square (faded sign, 'Via Pennina'; red/white CAI sign, Route 27). The road descends, passes under a road bridge and, after 200m/yds, becomes concrete, then stone steps. At the foot of the steps, turn right over a narrow footbridge (with an unpleasant drop to the left) and then climb some rough concrete steps. • On reaching the road, turn left. Follow the road to its end in 500m/yds, where it descends below the Grotta Biscotta and becomes a mule track (↦). Enjoying wide views down to the left, follow the track for 1km/ 0.6mi to the Colle la Serra — a junction of wide mule tracks, by a crucifix on the garden wall of a white house.

28b Colle la Serra to Bomerano
Time: 1h; *Grade:* easy, with a *height gain* of 60m/200ft

At the Colle la Serra, with the crucifix on your right, take the wide mule track going half left. This mostly-level path traverses the hillside, with wide views down to the right. After 1km/0.6mi you reach broad concrete steps (↦) below the Grotta Biscotta. The steps merge with a road, which you follow for 500m/yds, watching for rough narrow concrete steps going down to the right. • Descend these steps and cross a narrow footbridge *carefully* (unpleasant drop to the right). Join a track which ascends to the left. Follow this for 200m/yds up to the main piazza of Bomerano. The SITA bus to Amalfi stops here.

Terraced hillside above Marina di Furore (Walk segment 33)

29 Vèttica Maggiore — San Domenico

The monastery of San Domenico rises on a rocky promontory high above the coast, overlooking Vèttica and Positano. Our excellent path passes the Fourteen Stations of the Cross as it ascends. The monastery is still home to a handful of monks and I was concerned that mention in a book might bring an unwelcome stream of visitors. They assured me: 'This church is always open to those who seek peace in their hearts.' The church is barely furnished but has pleasant, old, if somewhat damaged frescoes. Outside, a shady patio with ↦ commands out-standing views down to Positano and along the coast — a splendid picnic spot. The path lies largely in shade before noon. There is a ↦ in an alley just below Vèttica's church. **Photographs pages 2, 72-73**

Time: 2h30min for the circuit; *Grade:* moderate, with a *height gain of 230m/750ft*

Starting from the main coast road just above Vèttica church, in the small piazza (G Gagliano) with a fountain, climb the steps (Via F Russo). After 40m/yds turn left into an alley that takes you by easy stages up to a T-junction with a horizontal alley. Turn left here. After about 100m/yds the path goes up gentle steps between houses, until it finally rounds a corner beyond the last house, and San Domenico comes into view high up on the hillside (↦ here). • After a short level section, take the well-built steps signposted to San Domenico; these lead up to the monas-tery. • Return the same way, noting the following options. ① To descend quickly to the coast road, take the first right turn after the first level section among the houses. ② To extend the walk along the coast through Praiano and come down to the coast road further east, once among the houses, continue east along the alley. It starts out level, rises gently between houses for 200m/yds, and then breaks out onto a road. Continue straight ahead on another road, downhill and round a bend to the left, then keep left on another road. This ends after about 400m/yds. Continue ahead on a path (Piazza San Luca) to the church of San Luca, in a large piazza overlooking the coast. • Continue between the church and its campanile. This path contours the coast, descending gradually, at one point going under a ceramic mural set into an arch. Soon you reach the Piazza Moressa (↤↦): continue ahead on a level path, to a small chapel. To descend to the coast road now, either take the alley before the chapel, or one of two alleys beyond it.

30 Bomerano to the Caserma Forestale

*This high traverse of the flanks of the loftiest of the Lattari Mountains offers immensely rewarding views over much of the peninsula — and, on a good day, distant Capri. There is many a bird's-eye view onto parts of the Sentiero degli Dei followed in Walk segment 26 and, in places, the surrounding escarpments are imposing, with 300m/1000ft-high cliffs above and below you. • This route is only for well-equipped, well-shod, experienced hill walkers who do not suffer from vertigo. With care, the route is quite easy to follow, even in mist and even without a map, but do not try it in wet or icy conditions: one section, although along a well-made mule track, skirts frighteningly-long, sheer drops. Moreover, in a couple of places the track goes over bare rock that could become slippery. There is no public ↤↦ in Bomerano, nor any drinking water en route. **Photograph pages 78-79***

Time: 4h50min; *Grade:* strenuous, with a *height gain* of 430m/1410ft

Facing the church in Bomerano, go right. Fork left after 100m/yds (Via Iovieno). After another 100m/yds, fork left again, uphill. After a further 100m/yds go across crossroads; 200m/yds further on, the road bends sharp left. Continue along it for another 200m/yds, then turn right up steps; they lead across a minor road to a higher road, where you turn left. • Follow this higher road, through some zigzags, up the left flank of the mountainside. When the road bends left, take rough steps straight ahead; this short-cut takes you up over a small col, on the far side of which you regain the road. Continue until the road ends and becomes a track (red/white CAI sign, 'Route 41'). Follow the track and, when it ends, the path running off it. The path, well waymarked with red paint dots, bends right up the hillside. Follow these waymarks up the hillside for 600m/0.35mi, to a prominent col (Capo Muro; 1072m/3500ft). *Note:* From this point on, the route always has the hillside up to the right, apart from some minor zigzags. • Follow a good, level mule track to the left (now with red/white CAI waymarks). This bends round to the left, until the slope up to the right becomes very slight. Here, 600m/0.35mi from Capo Muro, the mule track splits into many strands: follow the CAI waymarks downhill and generally to the right, between shrubs, for about 500m/yds. *Be very careful to keep to the waymarks.* They are frequent, but the path twists and turns among shrubs. *If you loose the waymarks, go back immediately to the one last seen* and look again or you are likely to get lost. • Eventually the waymarks lead you to a clear level mule track that takes you round to the right. You enter an imposing, steep rocky gorge-like valley — the 'exposed' section of the route, with sheer drops, mentioned in the introduction. It's exhilarating! The track contours the walls of the valley on wide rock ledges for about 1km/0.6mi. • Shortly after emerging from the confines of the valley, you reach a fine viewpoint named 'I Trasiti' (see photograph pages 78-79). From this viewpoint a well-built path leads gently down to the Caserma Forestale, a solid stone building with grilles over its windows.

31 Vèttica Maggiore (or Praiano) — Vallone di Praia

This walk segment is the first of three that provide connections between Vèttica Maggiore, Bomerano and Marina di Furore. This route takes you by easy stages to the central connecting point in the Vallone di Praia, a steep wooded valley to the east of Vèttica with fine views. It goes by easy stages up through the houses of Vèttica and Praiano, from where an excellent mule track leads up the side and head of the valley to a lone house at the start of a road. **Photograph pages 72-73**

31a Vèttica Maggiore to Vallone di Praia

Time: 1h15min; *Grade:* moderate, with a *height gain* of 220m/720ft
Starting from the main coast road just above Vèttica church, follow **Walk segment 27b** (page 72) as far as the chapel with the splendid view. • Take the path to the right of the chapel; it descends gradually for 150m/yds. Below you can now see the piazza from which access to Praiano's large white church, San Luca, can be gained — worth a detour. [Those based in Praiano can reach this point from their large church by taking the alley that goes between the church and the campanile. Turn left behind the church, to ascend steeply to this alley and turn right along it.] • The alley now rises gently, affording wider views. [After 400m/yds it comes alongside the road from which **Walk segment 27a** connects by steps.] • Soon the last house is reached, and the earthen (sometimes stony) mule track begins. After about 300m/yds, at a fork, keep left on the gently-rising path. For 1.5km/1mi this path traverses the left-hand side and head of the valley, always with the hillside up to the left, and almost always rising

— quite steeply for short stretches. Do *not* be tempted to take the steep steps going up to the left in two places. Eventually you reach the start of a motor road, by a house.

31b Vallone di Praia to Vèttica Maggiore
Time: 1h; *Grade:* easy

From the end of the road by a lone house, take the rough mule track uphill. It soon levels out, then makes a wide gradual sweep down the right-hand side of the valley, with the hillside up to your right. After 1km/0.6mi the path (now concreted) leads into Praiano. Keep ahead until the large church is visible down to the left, then follow **Walk segment 27a** (page 72) to Vèttica Maggiore.

32 Vallone di Praia — Bomerano

This segment connects the junction in the Vallone di Praia with Bomerano, high up on the Agerola plain. It continues up the wild valley, first visiting the remote but beautifully-sited church of Sant'Alfonso di Liguori — an idyllic picnic spot. Further up, the path skirts the foot of imposing cliffs containing caves with medieval masonry. Apart from two short indistinct stretches, the paths are good, although by the caves damage by mules makes boots essential. This part of the walk would probably be unpleasant in wet weather.

32a Vallone di Praia to Bomerano
Time: 2h; *Grade:* strenuous, with a *height gain* of 310m/1740ft

From the start of the motor road by a lone house, walk down the road for 200m/yds, to a building on the left with

Walk segment 30: From this rock ledge, 'I Trasiti', your views stretch along the coast as far as Capri, with Ischia off to the right. Nocelle lies below, and Positano is seen on the coast. Note that even if you have little walking experience, the beautifully constructed paths of Walk segment 22 will, on a fine day, lead you here safely.

three arched roll-door garages numbered 4, 6 and 8. Go up the concrete 'steps' (more like footholds!) on rocks to the left of the house. You pass a higher, abandoned building above the house. The increasingly-faint path leads through woodland and to the right of a few terraces. Look now for the start of a wide concrete path and climb it up to the chapel of Sant'Alfonso, already visible above.
• The path continues above the chapel to the foot of the cliffs: turn left here, still on a good path. It leads to a small col between the mountain on the right and an outlying rocky knoll. Beyond here the path is faint for about 100m/yds, until it joins a well-used mule track. Follow this rough track up to the foot of the higher cliffs and on to Bomerano — always with the hillside up to the right.

32b Bomerano to Vallone di Praia
Time: 1h30min; Grade: easy

Facing the large church in Bomerano, take the narrow road going left out of the square (faded sign, 'Via Pennina'; red/white CAI sign, Route 27). The road descends, passes under a road bridge and, after 200m/yds, becomes concrete, then stone steps. At the foot of the steps, continue straight ahead down a well-used earthen path along the valley floor. Soon the view down to the coast opens up, and the path, steep and broken, starts descending to the left, under imposing cliffs and caves. Keep left at two path junctions, ignoring paths down to the right. At a third junction, descend a few large rough-hewn steps, then go gently uphill on a faint path for 100m/yds, to a small col between the mountain on the left and an outlying rocky knoll. • Beyond the col, a fine path (soon concreted) continues to a junction at the foot of cliffs. Here turn sharp right, to descend to the chapel of Sant'Alfonso. Concrete steps continue below the chapel, then suddenly end: follow the faint path down to the left of some terraces and through light woodland (the last section, near a house, leads steeply down over rocks). On reaching a wide road, turn right. The road ends after 200m/yds by a lone house.

33 Vallone di Praia to Marina di Furore

Bus passengers whizzing along the coast get a subliminal glimpse of the Furore 'fjord' as they cross the bridge over a chasm before plunging into the next tunnel. Although some buildings and a bit of beach can be seen, there is no chance to work out what the place is really like. Marina di Furore is the harbour that once served the hillside village of Furore. This route takes you to the Marina, firstly along a short stretch of quiet road to Furore (noted, incidentally, for its fine white wine), then on steps descending to the small village of Sant'Elia. From here little-used, but excellently-built steps lead you gently down a wild hillside to the chasm of the Marina. **Photograph page 75**

Time: 2h; *Grade:* easy

From its start, follow the road for 800m/0.5mi, round two sharp bends to the left. Some 100m/yds beyond the second bend, take steep steps down to the right, after 300m/yds coming to a minor road. Turn right here to the finely-situated chapel of Sant'Elia and, beyond it, a viewpoint with seats. (Do *not* be tempted here by the CAI sign indicating a path to Praiano; it is reported to be 'difficult'.) • Return to the well-built steps and descend them. They lead across a wild hillside of open wood and abandoned terraces, down to the Marina. (Just before the final descent into the chasm, you could turn right, straight down to the road. It is worth turning right at this point in any case, to a good viewpoint part-way down. But I would not recommend the route all the way down to the marina itself because, though romantic, it is somewhat malodorous.) • At the road, you can take the bus to your resort. Gluttons for more punishment may wish to walk left along the road for 600m/0.35mi, to the next left-hand bend. From here a steep set of steps rises 120m/400ft, to the western end of Conca dei Marini. There you can turn right to a small chapel and a lovely traverse of Conca, picking up **Walk segment 36a** at the second church (San Antonio).

Conca dei Marini

This small area covers the hillside between the coast at Conca and the lip of the Agerola Plain at San Lazzaro; it is bounded on the west by the chasm of Furore and on the east by the chapel of Lone.

Getting about

Buses. The coast road is served by the Amalfi/Sorrento route. The Amalfi/Agerola route serves San Lazzaro and, on the way up, passes Vèttica Minore and the former convent of Santa Rosa. Tovere is served infrequently by a direct bus from Amalfi.

Tourist sight

The church of San Pancrazio at Conca is finely situated.

The coast east to Amalfi, seen from a small piazza in Conca dei Marini (Walk segments 36 and 37; Excursion 10)

Walk planning tips

By taking a bus to San Lazzaro in Agerola (check the timetables; not all Agerola buses go all the way) you gain easy access to the top of the steep hillside above Tovere and Conca dei Marini. These villages can then be reached on Walk segments 34a and 36a. There is also a splendid path back to Amalfi (Walk segments 34a and 35b), which must have been the route from the high plain of Agerola to Amalfi before the motor road was built. Or, in the reverse direction, instead of taking the bus from Amalfi, you could walk from there — at the cost of some climbing (Walk segments 35a and 36a). At the end of Walk segment 36a, consider descending on Walk segment 38 down to Spiaggia di Conca, a delightful little seaside village with a small beach (bar/restaurants in summer).

WALK SEGMENTS

34 San Lazzaro — Tovere (east side)
This short segment connects San Lazzaro to an important path junction on the hillside on the east side of Tovere.

34a San Lazzaro to Tovere (east side)
Time: 25min; *Grade:* easy, with a *descent* of 230m/750ft

From the main square in San Lazzaro take the road down to the edge of the plateau. Here, just as the road bends right, steps descend left. Follow these downhill through open countryside for 300m/yds, to a path junction. Turn left and continue downhill, behind a house and past a pylon, from where there are fine views left along the coast to Amalfi. You reach a path junction marked by a cube-shaped concrete water supply building.

34b Tovere (east side) to San Lazzaro
Time: 40min; *Grade:* moderate, with a *height gain* of 200m/660ft

From the junction by the water supply building ascend the steps, past a pylon (fine views right along the coast to Amalfi) and a house. Some 500m/yds from the start, turn right at another junction, to ascend steps to San Lazzaro.

35 Amalfi road tunnel (west end) — Tovere (east side)
This route provides the essential link between Amalfi and the Conca dei Marini hillside, with minimal road-walking. Affording extensive views, it passes through pleasant villages, under the brooding presence of the Santa Rosa Convent on its rocky perch to the west. You could eliminate some of the walking by taking the Agerola bus as far as Vèttica Minore and pick up the route from there.

35a Amalfi road tunnel (west end) to Tovere (east side)
Time: 2h20min; *Grade:* moderate, with a *height gain* of 380m/1250ft

From the western end of the road tunnel, take the narrow

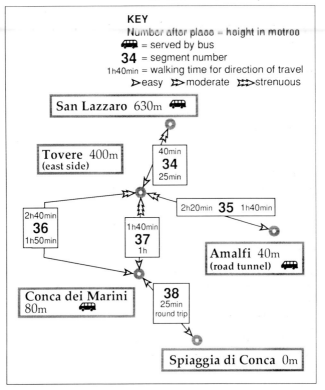

KEY
Number after place = height in metres
 = served by bus
34 = segment number
1h40min = walking time for direction of travel
▷easy ▷▷moderate ▷▷▷strenuous

San Lazzaro 630m
Tovere 400m (east side)
40min **34** 25min
2h40min **36** 1h50min
1h40min **37** 1h
2h20min **35** 1h40min
Amalfi 40m (road tunnel)
Conca dei Marini 80m
38 25min round trip
Spiaggia di Conca 0m

road (Via Maestra dei Villaggi) that rises gently between apartments. It shortly narrows into a path which is followed for 1.5km/1mi (generally uphill) to Lone's cemetery. En route you pass the small chapel of La Carmine and a balcony look-out under Lone's chapel; soon after this latter, the path bends right; at the cemetery the path turns left and descends very steeply to the Agerola road. • Turn right up the road, round the bend to the left and, at the next right-hand bend, take the path uphill to the left (Salita San Pietro a Gudaro). Very soon go right, climbing up more steps. These lead up and round to the left, to the church of San Michele at Vèttica Minore. Go below the church up to the road. • Turn left on the road for 40m/yds, then go right up more steps (Via Maestra dei Villaggi; ignore the 'privato' sign). Take steps up to cross a minor road, and then follow broad zigzags up the mountainside. [After about 500m/yds, you can take a short-cut to Conca. When you see metal railings on the right, go left, initially on a broad concrete shelf, to join

Great bushes of tree-spurge (Euphorbia dendroides) light up many walks. These can grow up to 2m/6ft in height.

Walk segment 37a after 300m/yds; see page 86]. The main path (badly broken for a stretch) makes a broad sweep up to the left, to a path junction by a concrete water supply building.

35b Tovere (east side) to the Amalfi road tunnel (west end)
Time: 1h40min; Grade: easy, with a descent of 250m/820ft
From the path junction by a concrete water supply building, looking downhill, take the path descending left across the open hillside. Badly broken for a stretch, it later leads in broad zigzags down to a minor road and then down a few more steps to the Agerola road at Vèttica Minore. • Turn left along the road for 40m/yds, then right to pass below the church of San Michele. At first level, the path then descends to the right, to a T-junction. Here turn left to reach the road again. Turn right down the road, go round the bend to the right and, just past the cemetery, take steep steps up to the left. • At the top of the steps turn right; after about 1.5km/1mi (generally descending), you reach the road tunnel.

36 Tovere (east side) — Conca dei Marini
This segment wanders pleasantly across the hillside above Conca, as far as the rim of the deep ravine of Furore to the west; it then returns to Conca on a lower path. Photograph page 81

36a Tovere (east side) to Conca dei Marini
Time: 1h50min; Grade: easy, with a descent of 200m/660ft
From the path junction by a concrete water supply building, looking downhill, take the level path to the right. It ascends gradually and becomes a narrow road. Some 400m/yds from the start pass a ↔ on the left. [**Walk segment 37a** descends steps to the left here.] After passing a small chapel on the left, turn left down a wide road. • Follow this road, with little traffic, past a church on the right, counting the 14 Stations of the Cross beside the road. Three hairpin bends take you down to the Amalfi/Agerola road: turn left. • After 200m/yds, on a left-hand bend, take steps down to the right (between two houses, Nos 63 and 65). You descend through light woods, with

views across the Furore valley to Praiano — a pleasant picnic spot. At the foot of the steps you join a level path by houses. After 300m/yds, this path turns right and descends to a minor road: turn left. • Follow the road for 400m/yds, to the church of San Antonio on the right. (Just before the church there is an ornate ⭢⭢ on the left, worked by a lever on the right.) Turn right onto the path beside the church for some wonderful coastal views; after 200m/yds you rejoin the road. Some 200m/yds further on, ignore the first steps down to the right; take the second flight, a little further on. These lead down to a fine view of the coast towards Amalfi and then to the church of San Pancrazio, with its commanding viewpoint to the west. • From the viewpoint, take the road, then use the path on the right to descend 150m/yds down to the coast road at Conca, by the Hotel Belvedere. (In summer, when the hotel is open, the Reception sells SITA tickets.)

36b Conca dei Marini to Tovere (east side)
Time: 2h40min; *Grade:* moderate, with a *height gain* of 320m/1050ft

From the Hotel Belvedere on the coast road at Conca, climb steps, and then a minor road, for 150m/yds, up to the church of San Pancrazio and its commanding viewpoint to the west. • From the upper side of the church (⭢⭢), take gentle steps up to a minor road, where you continue to the right, up to a viewpoint to the east. Continue up steps for some 200m/yds to a minor road and turn left. [**Walk segment 37b** continues up steps here.] After 200m/yds take a few steps down left, to a stretch of level path (wonderful coast views) and the church of San Antonio. • Follow the adjacent road to the left for 400m/yds, then turn right up a steep flight of steps (at a right angle to the road, between houses). Beyond the houses, this path turns left and, after a level stretch, climbs steps to the main Amalfi/Agerola road. Turn left here. • After 200m/yds turn right up the Tovere road and follow it past three hairpin bends, the 14 Stations of the Cross, and a church on the left. Go 400m/yds past the church, then take a very narrow, level road off to the right. Follow this for 600m/0.35mi, to a path junction with a concrete water supply building.

37 Tovere (east side) — Conca dei Marini
More direct than segment 36, this route goes past the prominently-sited former convent of Santa Rosa, now an hotel. **Photograph page 81**

37a Tovere (east side) to Conca dei Marini
Time: 1h; *Grade:* easy, with a *descent* of 320m/1050ft

Follow **Walk segment 36a** opposite to the ⭢⭢ on the left;

here take steps downhill. • After 100m/yds the path turns left and traverses a wild hillside, until it reaches a steeper slope overlooking the coast to Amalfi in the east. [The narrow short-cut path mentioned in **Walk segment 35a** comes in here.] The path now turns straight downhill to the old Santa Rosa building. • Cross the road by the road tunnel and take the minor road signposted to Conca. Follow this for 500m/yds; just after you pass a high cliff on the right, take steps down to the left. • The steps level out by a fine viewpoint to the east, at a minor road. Follow the road for 50m/yds, then descend a final flight of steps to the church of San Pancrazio with its commanding viewpoint to the west. • From the viewpoint, take the road, then use the path on the right to descend 150m/yds down to the coast road at Conca, by the Hotel Belvedere. (In summer, when the hotel is open, the Reception sells SITA tickets.)

37b Conca dei Marini to Tovere (east side)
Time: 1h40min; *Grade:* strenuous, with a *height gain* of 320m/1050ft
Follow **Walk segment 36b** (page 85) past the viewpoint to the east and up steps to the road, where that segment turns left. Continue up steps to a higher road and there turn right. After 500m/yds you come to the old convent of Santa Rosa, now an hotel. Cross the road just by the road tunnel and take the steps that lead up above the tunnel. Then continue up the hillside, with splendid views to the east towards Amalfi and beyond. • After about 200m/yds, the path turns left. [Here you could take a short-cut to **Walk segment 35b** (just below the broken stretch of path): follow the small footpath to the right; it sweeps round the hillside, descending gradually, until it meets the well-built path descending to the right.] Our path now turns left, traverses a wild hillside for 400m/yds, and then turns up to the right. You join a narrow road by a ••; turn right. After 400m/yds you reach a path junction with a concrete water supply building.

38 Conca dei Marini — Spiaggia di Conca dei Marini
We visit the seaside village mentioned in the Walk planning tips.
Time: 25min round trip; *Grade:* easy, with a *height gain* of 80m/260ft
Take the steps down from the coast road on the left side of the Hotel Belvedere at Conca. These lead down to a delightful fishing hamlet and a small beach, where there are two bar/restaurants (open all day, but only from mid-May to the end of September). The sun leaves the beach mid-afternoon. Return to the road by the same route.

Maiori/Minori

From each of these small towns a deep valley runs from the coast into the hinterland; the valleys are separated by a wooded ridge bearing the ruined convent of San Nicola. The Sambuco Valley behind Minori is only 4km/2.5mi long, ending at the mountain pass, Il Passo. The valley behind Maiori opens out after 6km/3.7mi to the wide undulating plain of Tramonti (photographs pages 32-33 and 136), itself divided by a ridge at the end which the cemetery of Santa Maria looks out over the region's 'capital', Polvica. Tramonti and the area to the east is ringed by a rugged ridge of high mountains. On the most southerly of these, at a height of 870m/2900ft, is perched the Santuario dell'Avvocata, shown on page 97.

Getting about

The towns are served by the coastal service Amalfi/Salerno. SITA also runs a service from Maiori to Tramonti, see details in Walk segments 43 and 44.

Overlooking the sea, this small piazza by the 10th-century church of San Michele, lies on the path between Maiori and Minori (Walk segment 39 Excursion 9).

Tourist sights

Minori. Apart from the remains of a Roman villa with some fine mosaics, there is also a splendid large basilica on the east side of town, by the shady Piazza Cantilena.

Maiori. Some 4km/2.5mi along the coast road from Maiori towards Salerno a former abbey, Santa Maria de Olearia, houses some quite outstanding frescoes dating from the 12th century. See details in Walk segment 41.

WALK SEGMENTS

39 Minori — Maiori

A good path connects these towns, so that you can walk between them away from the busy coast road. It climbs quite high, but gives excellent views down to Minori and visits the 10th-century church of San Michele, with its little piazza looking out to sea. **Photograph page 87**

39a Minori to Maiori

Time: 1h; *Grade:* moderate, with a *height gain* of 140m/460ft

From the basilica set back off the eastern end of Minori's promenade, take the road under its tower, walking away from the coast. After 200m/yds, just past a modern school on the right, turn right up well-built steps. Beyond a few zigzags (➡➡), you come to a junction. Turn right (signposted to Convento San Nicola, San Michele, Maiori). Some 100m/yds further on there is an excellent viewpoint (➡➡) over Minori. Continue up more steps to the church of San Michele (you are now in the hamlet of Torre). Continue to left of the church, bend to the left, then go up more steps, to a prominent junction by railings. [**Walk segment 42** goes up left here.] • Continue on a generally level path, through a wide right-hand bend; then descend into Maiori. On coming to a large church, go right round the back of it and descend to the main road, then turn right to the sea-front.

39b Maiori to Minori

Time: 1h; *Grade:* moderate, with a *height gain* of 140m/460ft

From the statue of Mother and Child on the sea-front in Maiori, follow the broad road inland for 200m/yds, to a small triangular piazza on the left (Raffaele d'Amato). Turn left, ascend to the right of the large church, and continue up the path (Via Vena), gently climbing the hillside. The path rises for 400m/yds, then bends right into a side-valley. After sweeping round to the far side of the valley, you come to a prominent junction by railings. [**Walk segment 42** goes up to the right here.] • The path to Minori continues ahead and soon bends right to the church of San Michele. Continue down to a fine

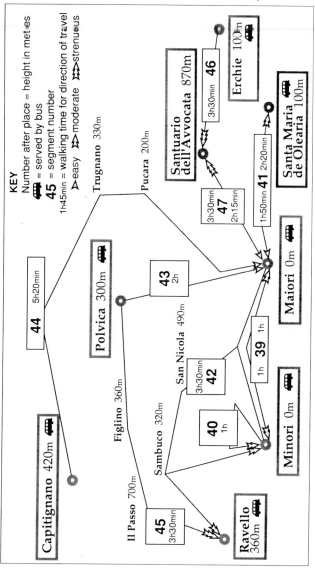

KEY

Number after place = height in metres

🚌 = served by bus

45 = segment number

1h45min = walking time for direction of travel
➤easy ➤➤moderate ➤➤➤strenuous

Capitignano 420m 🚌

Polvica 300m 🚌

Figlino 360m

Il Passo 700m

San Nicola 490m

Sambuco 320m

Ravello 360m 🚌

Trugnano 330m

Pucara 200m

Santuario dell'Avvocata 870m

Erchie 100m 🚌

Santa Maria de Olearia 100m 🚌

Maiori 0m 🚌

Minori 0m 🚌

44 5h20min

43 2h

42 3h30min

40 1h

45 3h30min

39 1h

41 1h50min 2h20min

47 3h30min 2h15min

46 3h30min

1h   1h

viewpoint (••) above Minori and to the town. On reaching a road, turn left to the basilica and Piazza Cantilena.

40 Minori Circuit

If you have an hour to spare and would like to get good view of Minori and its setting, then this circuit is ideal.

Time: 1h; *Grade:* moderate, with a *height gain* of 150m/500ft

From the basilica set back off the eastern end of Minori's

promenade, take the road under its tower, walking away from the coast. After 200m/yds, just past a modern school on the right, turn right up well-built steps. Beyond a few zigzags (••), you come to a junction. Continue uphill to the left (Via Torre Annunziata). The path soon steepens and climbs a long flight of steps. After passing an old tower, you come to a bend to the left. • Almost immediately, turn left on a gently-descending path. This sweeps to the left for 300m/yds, giving a bird's-eye view of Minori and the hillside up to Ravello. After going into and out of the side-valley and descending some steps, you come to a prominent junction. You can descend to the left here but, to extend the walk a little further, go right uphill for a short way, then follow the path down to a motor road in the town and turn left to the sea-front.

41 Maiori — Santa Maria de Olearia

The frescoes in the 12th-century monastery of Santa Maria give a splendid focus to this walk. The monastery was founded by monks who came from the eastern Mediterranean, and the frescoes echo the style of those seen, for example, in Meteor, Greece. You can take the bus to the monastery or back, if you wish; the bus stop bears the name of the monastery and is the next stop after Maiori cemetery, some 4km along the road to Salerno from Maiori. The opening hours are as yet undecided, but will probably be 09.00-12.00 and 16.00-18.00 (check at the AST near the eastern end of the sea-front in Maiori). If the monastery is closed, Signor 'Vincenzo' in the house next door to the building is a keyholder and is usually willing to let visitors in, there being no charge. The walk itself takes a route parallel with the coast road and high above it, mostly on a mule track; it traverses a wild hillside of myrtle and white heather, with extensive views along the coast. Photograph page 14

41a Maiori to Santa Maria de Olearia

Time: 2h20min; Grade: moderate, with a height gain of 260m/850ft
From the Bar Oriente near the eastern end of the sea-front in Maiori, follow the road inland for 200m/yds. Where the road bends left, fork right into Via de Iosola. After 100m/yds, at a T-junction, turn right; 30m/yds further on, by a ••, turn left up Via Grade dei Pezzi. By always ascending and taking the obvious path ahead, you emerge from the houses, swing to the right and climb (with a wall on the right), after 800m/0.5mi coming to a prominently-sited isolated pink and white house (No 5).
• Pass the house [**Walk segment 47b** leaves up steps to the left.] Continue on the now-level path, which will contour into and out of the next wide side-valley, rising and falling slightly. You will emerge at a fork of tracks 1.2km/0.7mi further on — it can already been seen ahead, on the same contour. On reaching the fork, go left uphill on a wide mule track. Already high above the coast

road, this track climbs another 400m/yds, up to a junction by low woven-wattle walls retaining the hillside. Continue round to the right, soon beginning a gradual descent. After a further 1km/0.6mi along the wide mule track, you reach a house by some abandoned cars. You have passed above Maiori's cemetery. • Just beside the house, take the track that descends quite steeply; initially it runs straight down the hillside, then bends to the right. After 150m/yds, you come to a lower wide mule track. Follow it to the right, down some zigzags, to the coast road. Turn left and walk into a side-valley. The monastery of Santa Maria de Olearia is on the left, 300m/yds beyond the second bend in the side-valley.

41b Santa Maria de Olearia to Maiori

Time: 1h50min; *Grade:* easy, with a *height gain* of 120m/395ft and a descent of 200m/660ft

Turn right out of the monastery of Santa Maria, to descend the coast road for 300m/yds through a side valley. Go round two left-hand bends: 100m/yds beyond the second bend, climb a short flight of steps up to the right. The path leads past a lime kiln to a steep mule track which takes you in zigzags up the hillside for 200m/yds. The track then swings right and climbs more gently by some burnt pine trees; on leaving these, where the main track bends right, climb the steep rocky track straight ahead. This bends right and leads after 150m/yds to a higher wide mule track, by a house and some abandoned cars. • Turn left here. The track now contours the hillside ascending gently for 1km/0.6mi, to a fork by low woven-wattle walls retaining the hillside. Go left now, gently downhill. In a further 400m/yds the path descends to a narrow gravel road, at the start of a wide side-valley. Continue to the right. This road (later reverting to path) will contour into and out of the side-valley for 1.2km/0.7mi, emerging on by the isolated pink and white house which can be seen ahead. [**Walk segment 47a** joins here.] • On reaching the house, descend the steps beyond it, bending to the right. Descend for 800m/0.5mi, always keeping ahead at the few junctions encountered. You arrive in Maiori: descend steps between houses for 100m/yds, turn right at a junction by a ➤ and, after a further 30m/yds, go left on Via de Iosola. This leads to a road to the sea-front.

42 Minori or Maiori — San Nicola — Sambuco — Ravello or Minori

The now-abandoned convent of San Nicola sits on a high hilltop above Minori and Maiori, looking out over the Bay of Salerno and ringed by

higher mountains. A good path makes its way quite easily from Minori or Maiori up to the building, although the climb is relatively prolonged Having enjoyed the view from the convent, you can either retrace your steps or go on to the pleasant little farming village of Sambuco and take a valley walk back to Minori. From Sambuco you also have the option of taking the minor road to Ravello.

Time: 3h30min; *Grade:* moderate, with a *height gain* of 490m/1600ft

Take **Walk segment 39a** (from Minori) or **39b** (from Maiori) to the path starting at the railings. Turn uphill. • You now stay on this path for about 2km/1.2mi, often climbing steps, keeping near the top of the ridge or on its left side, moving from housing into pine and then other woods. Excellent views accompany you. Eventually, having passed below and to the left of San Nicola, you come to the top of the climb. Here turn sharp right for 400m/yds, to reach the convent and admire the view, then return to the main path. Here turn sharp left to return the way you came. • Or, to continue via Sambuco, turn half right here, on a broad level track along the ridge. After 300m/yds, at a ruined building, turn half left down a prominent mule track; it takes you down to the stream below Sambuco and up concrete steps to the road. • Turn left for 400m/yds along the road to a SITA bus stop and turning place. From here you could continue along the road to Ravello. To descend to Minori, after 50m/yds on the road fork left down a path. This leads to steps that are the start of the path down the valley back to Minori. Just keep straight ahead all the way. When you meet the first road in Minori, turn left, then go right round a bend and follow the road straight ahead through the town, to the coast road. The last turning on the left before the promenade leads into the shady Piazza Cantilena in front of the basilica.

43 Polvica to Maiori

Walk segments 43, 44 and 45 explore the high farming area of Tramonti. Here you are away from the coast, ringed by high mountains, and the area has a quite different feel about it. For one thing the risk of winter frost forbids growth of the ubiquitous lemon trees of the coast; here you see only vines on the pergolas. The viticulture demonstrates self-sufficiency: by each vineyard you will see willow stumps, the new fronds being clipped each autumn to bind the vines to the pergolas. The pergolas themselves come from the mountainsides, where you will see large areas of coppiced chestnut and alder, grown just to provide this sort of timber, and enormous stockpiles of harvested poles (see photograph on pages 32-33). Not only fruit, but vegetables are grown. You see all sorts of vegetables in the small fields — aubergines, peppers, and many kinds of beans. In autumn tomatoes will be hung to dry. Everywhere the small three-wheeler 'scooter' lorry is to be seen, which has largely, but not completely, supplanted the mule. • This walk takes you in easy stages from the 'capital' of Tramonti down to the coast at Maiori and gives you a good feel for the area. Perhaps half the distance is covered on almost traffic-free minor roads. Walk segment 44 provides a lengthier excursion and an even better insight, while Walk segment 45 takes you into the forested mountainsides. • To get to Polvica, take the Tramonti bus from outside the AST near the eastern end of the promenade in Maiori (SITA tickets from the Bar Oriente next door but one). The AST has up-to-date timetables. After the bus turns left off the main road to descend and climb out of a small gorge, alight immediately on reaching houses; this is Polvica. **Photographs below and page 136**

Time: 2h; *Grade:* easy

Taking the bus driver's view as you enter Polvica, take the first road immediately on the left (by a clock and a sign denoting a speed limit of 30km/h). This bends right after 100m/yds and descends to a bridge. Just after the

Lemon trees overhang a typical narrow road in a lower part of the Tramonti region (Walk segment 43)

bridge, take the path up left; at a fence, go half right. On regaining the road, turn left. [**Walk segment 45** goes right up the narrow road here.] • Now keeping on the right-hand side of the valley, follow the wider road for 1km/0.6mi. At a fork just before a church, go left down a narrow road; pass below the church and, after 50m/yds, fork right, to ascend to a small square in Paterno San Arcangelo. Turn left to continue on a narrow road. From here the route, alternating between path and road, will wind into and out of four successive side-valleys on the right. • After 50m/yds, at a T-junction, turn right. Follow the narrow road into and out of the first side-valley. On reaching the highest point in the road, continue for 100m/yds, to where the road turns sharp left and ends by a house. Here go straight downhill on rough stone steps. After 150m/yds, at a T-junction, turn right and take a path into and out of the second side valley. As you come up to the church of Paterno Sant'Elia, there is a splendid picnic spot in a small piazza, complete with seats in sun or shade, ↦ and magnificent view. • Past the church, join a wide but rough road and follow it for 600m/0.35mi, to where it bends sharp left. Here take the path up to the right of the house and round the third side-valley. [Just before you reach the ridge bounding the south side of this valley, **Walk segment 44** joins from the left.] • Round the ridge to the right and take a path below a house. After 250m/yds, you come to the end of a terrace (on your right). Here descend steps half left and walk alongside a lower terrace. At its end, by a stout structure of poles, turn right and contour (gently descending) round the fourth side-valley, coming to the upper houses of Ponteprimario. Descend between the houses, always going left at junctions. At the bottom, turn left into the little piazza with its memorial to the citizens of the village lost to flooding in the mid-1950s (on a night after it had rained incessantly for 48 hours). Then turn right and descend the valley to Maiori, using the minor road which lies to the west of the main road. At one point this road is interrupted by a garden centre with large grille gates; the path goes right on top of a low wall to rejoin the road. As you descend, look up at the southernmost mountain on the eastern side, to spot the sanctuary of Avvocata (Walk segment 47) just below the summit.

44 Capitignano to Maiori

This all-day walk provides a very pleasant and easy, if lengthy, ramble through the backwaters of Tramonti, mostly on paths and tracks, and *always with the magnificent mountain backdrop. See Walk segment 43 (page 93) for general comments on Tramonti and its bus service. Buses from Maiori continue beyond Polvica to Capitignano, the terminus. Alight where the bus turns round. Sometimes the bus first makes a short detour right from Polvica up to Corsano and back, before continuing to Capitignano. **Photograph pages 32-33***

Time: 5h20min; Grade: easy, with a height gain of 300m/980ft in short stages

From Capitignano, go back down the bus route for about 50m/yds, then turn right (by a ➙) up a steep narrow paved road. After 200m/yds this changes into a mule track and sweeps to the right, to join a main road after a further 700m/0.4mi. From here take the minor road on the right; it is paved at the outset and then becomes gravel. Follow this for 2.6km/1.6mi along the crest of the ridge that splits the Tramonti Plain. You reach Santa Maria di Tramonti — a cemetery sited just at the end of the ridge. • From the cemetery, retrace your route for 10 minutes, to just before the point where the road goes downhill to the left; here take a mule track down to the right. On reaching a minor road, turn left. After 50m/yds go right, over a bridge, to hug the lower slopes of a hill. Some 50m/yds after passing a first house (on your right), turn right down a steep concrete road; after a further 50m/yds, turn left between houses. Shortly you find yourself on a pleasant path with an excellent embankment overlooking a stream — a pleasant picnic spot. The path continues down to the stream and curves up right to the houses of Trugnano. • Continue straight ahead within Trugnano; a road joins from left and after 300m/yds departs again to the left. Continue straight ahead down a narrow lane. After another 200m/yds you can see the ornate campanile and church in Campinola. The lane ends by gates. Turn left up steps and follow a paved path round to the right, under vine pergolas. On coming to a T-junction, turn right down a concrete track, until you are forced to go left beside the supporting wall of a vineyard, onto a narrow overgrown path. This crosses a small bridge and ultimately leads left up to a village (Casa Vaccaro) on the main road. • Follow the main road downhill for 800m/0.5mi, to the second bend to the right. Here turn left up a concrete lane (by a sign, 'Ponte'). Now follow the left-hand side of valley for 2km/1.2mi, contouring through the small villages of Gete, Pendolo, and Novella. The route varies from road to track to path. Finally you reach Pucara — its two church towers rise above the meadow on your approach. Take the steps down to the right just beyond the church, to rejoin the main road. • Turn left for 100m/yds, and then turn sharp right down a side road. [Instead, if you are short of time, you could continue on the main road for 1.3km/0.8mi and then turn right into the village of Ponteprimario; see **Walk segment 43**.] After 300m/yds of descent on this side-road, turn left in front of a paper mill (Carto-technica Civale), to cross an iron footbridge. Descend a few steps and then turn left down more steps, to the riverside path. Soon start climbing some modern steps. Just as they turn left and end, take the old path, ascending gently ahead. In a further 200m/yds, beyond a few zigzags, you come to a T-junction with a level path. Turn left here, and continue on **Walk segment 43**, page 94.

45 Polvica to Ravello

This walk has three contrasting sections: a stroll through the farming areas of Tramonti; a strenuous ascent on a rough mule track through chestnut woodland and wild hillside (with magnificent displays of cyclamen in September/October) up to the Ravello/Chiunzi (and Naples) road; then a leisurely walk down this road to Ravello, admiring the marvellous panorama of encircling mountains. Traffic is not at all oppressive, at least on weekdays, and the views more than compensate for the need to walk on tarmac. • The route-finding is quite clear, but the route should be undertaken only by confident, well-shod walkers, as the mule track 'feels' remote and is rough. For details of the bus service to Polvica see Walk segment 43, page 93.

Time: 3h30min; Grade: strenuous, with a height gain of 440m/1440ft
From Polvica follow **Walk segment 43** to where the narrow road turns off. Go up the road, to some houses. Pass to the left of the houses, rising to a higher, single-track road: turn right. After 600m/0.35mi you reach the village of Figlino. Follow the road straight through the village; arches span the entry and exit. • Some 100m/yds after the last house, turn left up a narrow road (with the 'Figlino' name-plate). On reaching some houses (the hamlet of Iasore), turn right; 50m/yds further on, turn left in front of a house, to take a track up the hill and into the forest. • On entering the forest the path bends left, after 50m/yds coming to a crossing of mule tracks: turn right. This path leaves the forest, contours between cultivated terraces, passes to the left of a fenced area, and then re-enters the forest. Join a prominent mule track immediately, ascending gently to the left. • You now ascend this track for 1.5km/1mi (about 1h), gaining 300m/1000ft in height. The route should always be obvious. Although you will come across junctions where paths diverge, the correct path is clear: it goes up the left-hand side of valley, contouring about 100m up from the stream, and it always

ascends gradually, with the hillside up to the left. There are three distinct sections: between mature old chestnuts; a rocky stretch through light scrub, sometimes with rough steps; a third section, again with large trees. Just before the final section, you may have to get by a large fallen tree.
• At the top of the path you come to the road at Il Passo: turn left. Now just amble down the road, enjoying the views. Down to the left lies the village of Sambuco (Walk segment 42), while the sanctuary of Avvocata (Walk segment 47) is silhouetted on a shelf just below the summit of the last far mountain on the left. Later, the nearer hilltop convent of San Nicola (Walk segment 42) comes into view. At the entrance to the Ravello road tunnel, keep left for the Amalfi bus stop and the town centre.

46 Erchie to Santuario dell'Avvocata

If you have spent any time near the coast east of Amalfi, you will have seen the large Avvocata monastery perched on its eyrie, a shelf just below the summit of the most easterly of the coastal mountains. It looks down on Maiori from a height of 873m/2860ft, beckoning any keen hill-walker. It opens at Pentecost for a service, and a few other times each year. • This route, and Walk segment 47, are recommended only for well-equipped, well-shod, experienced hill-walkers. Our route goes up from the coast road above the village of Erchie, some 8km east of Maiori. We follow a wooded valley up the east side of the mountain, to join the track that leads from Cava dei Tirreni to the monastery — with good views of Salerno, its bay, and mountains beyond. Once on the summit ridge, mountains to the north and west come into view, including Vesuvius. Walk segment 47 offers the routes up from and down to Maiori. **Photographs below and overleaf** • *The starting point from the road above Erchie is a little-used, unnamed SITA bus stop: show the bus driver this wording, to alight at the correct stop:*
PER FAVORE, CI PUÒ FAR SCHENDERE ALLA FERMATA TRA CAPO D'ORSO E ERCHIE, DOVE COMINCIA IL SENTIERO CHE VA ALL'AVVOCATA.
Time: 3h30min *Grade:* strenuous, with a *height gain* of 800m/2600ft

From the bus stop at Erchie take the mule track marked

The sanctuary of Avvocata lies on a shelf almost 900m/ 3000ft above the coast (Walk segments 46 and 47).

at its start with red/white CAI markings and details of routes to the Santuario dell'Avvocata and a *sorgente* (a spring which we will visit). We will take longer to get to the sanctuary than the time shown here, as ours is a longer and better route. Ascend the heavily-used path up the left-hand side of the valley to a ruin reached in **45min**. Just past this ruin, fork left, following the red/white waymarks. • At **1h** the path starts to descend. Here take the path uphill left; it bears red/white waymarks (as does the other, descending path). At **1h25min** you come to a four-way junction, from where you can see picnic tables, a shrine and a spring (the *sorgente*) down to the right. Ignore these and the path going sharp left, marked with a red spot (I have been told that the red/white marking continues on this, a rough path that leads directly up to the monastery). Keep straight ahead uphill on the well-used path, now waymarked with only an occasional red dot. The hillside is still on your left. • At **1h50min**, after climbing continuously, you round a bend to the left, the path gradient lessens, the woodland thins out, and a stream is seen only 20m/60ft down to the right, flowing parallel with the path. After about 200m/yds, take the path that crosses the stream and climbs half-right steeply up the hillside — a

Climbing high into the mountains on the way to Santuario dell'Avvocata, with views over the Bay of Salerno and the mountains beyond (Walk segment 46). Our route has zigzagged up from the bottom right-hand side of the picture to the crest of the brown ridge, which it has followed to meet this excellent mule track.

narrow rocky route. The path leaves the wood, bends to the right and then curves to the left, now less steep and rocky. About 200m/yds further on, just before you enter a grove of tall trees (**2h**), look for a definite, but narrow path turning sharp right. Take this earthen path straight up the hillside, then follow it in broad zigzags up to the ridge bounding the northeastern (right-hand) side of the valley. The cliffs and rounded summit of Monte Avvocata are towering over you on the other side of the valley. Follow the ridge up to the left, to meet a prominent mule track at a T-junction. • Turn left and follow the mule track, now with red/white waymarks, straight ahead up to the summit ridge (magnificent all-round views) and then briefly down the other side to the monastery (**3h30min**).

47 Santuario dell'Avvocata — Maiori
This much used but exceedingly rough path provides the direct connection between Maiori and the sanctuary.

47a Santuario dell'Avvocata to Maiori
Time: 2h15min; *Grade:* easy, with a *descent* of 800m/2600ft

Find the start of the steep descent path below the southern end of the monastery. It is marked liberally with yellow dots. Follow the waymarks on their tortuous route down

to a picnic site with a table in the woods on the left (**30min**). Continue down to the right on the main, heavily-used path — to a seat, a shrine and a spring (**40min**). Continue straight on down to an old lime kiln (**50min**), go round its lower end, and continue descending to a small grassy promontory, where there is a forlorn building with a double, rounded roof (**1h**). • Go down the narrow path on the right-hand side of the building, to the nearby valley floor, and cross the stream. For the next 50 minutes (1.2km/0.8mi) you will descend the right-hand side of this valley; an old water duct and two black plastic pipes accompany you on the right for much of the way. In its lower reaches the path passes cultivated terraces, but remains rocky. Finally, stark concrete steps take you down to an isolated pink and white house. From here take **Walk segment 41b** (page 91) down to Maiori.

47b Maiori to the Santuario dell'Avvocata
Time: 3h30min; *Grade:* strenuous, with a *height gain* of 900m/2950ft

Take **Walk segment 41a** (page 90) up to the pink and white house (**20min**). Pass to the right of the house and immediately take the concrete steps ascending to the left. At the top of them, you begin a long ascent up the left-hand side of the valley ahead. This climb, on a rocky path, lasts for 1h05min (1.2km/0.8mi); for much of the time an old water duct and two black plastic pipes accompany you on the left. Finally the path reaches the valley floor and then ascends the other side, to a small grassy promontory where there is an all-but-abandoned building with a double, rounded roof (**2h25min**). • Climb the heavily-used path directly behind the building, to reach an old lime kiln (**2h35min**), then a seat, a shrine and a spring (**2h45min**), and finally a picnic table on the right in the woods (**2h55min**). From here the path turns left and a liberal sprinkling of yellow spots guide you up to the Santuario dell'Avvocata.

The path from Fontanelle to Sant'Agata for a time goes high above the coast, with distant views along the peninsula (Walk segment 66, Sorrento area).

✳ Sorrento

The bustling town of Sorrento lies on a broad shelf 70m/230ft above the sea. To the south and west the terrain (both cultivated and wooded) rises quite steeply, eventually to a height of 400m/1300ft. Here, on the crest of the peninsula, lies the village of Sant'Agata. The ridge continues southwest to the tip of the peninsula, rising to a maximum height of 500m/1650ft at Monte San Costanzo, near the village of Termini. The elegant small town of Massa Lubrense sits a little above the coast, on the west of the peninsula.

As the slopes are less steep than on the Amalfi Coast, the paths here consist less often of steps. Moreover, the path network is now less complete, because road-building and other development has interrupted it in a number of places. However, the chosen segments take the most complete of the remaining paths and offer good walking. The paths south of Sant'Agata and Termini are much as they have always been, so the above comments do not apply to them. When it is wet, even on the easy paths, you will often need shoes with a good tread to prevent slipping on steep stone paving.

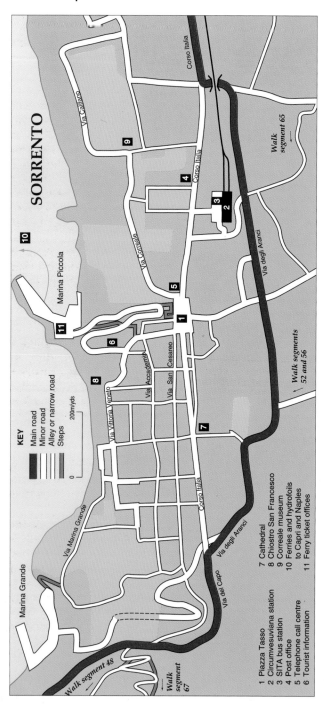

SORRENTO

KEY
Main road
Minor road
Alley or narrow road
Steps

0   200m/yds

Marina Grande

Via Marina Grande

Via del Capo

Via degli Aranci

Via Vittoria Veneto

Via Accademia

Via San Cesareo

Corso Italia

Via Correale

Corso Italia

Via Califano

Corso Italia

Via degli Aranci

Marina Piccola

Walk segment 65

Walk segments 52 and 56

Walk segment 48

Walk segment 67

1 Piazza Tasso
2 Circumvesuviana station
3 SITA bus station
4 Post office
5 Telephone call centre
6 Tourist information
7 Cathedral
8 Chiostro San Francesco
9 Correale museum
10 Ferries and hydrofoils
    to Capri and Naples
11 Ferry ticket offices

You may wish to obtain the excellent walking map with historical notes covering Massa Lubrense, Sorrento and Sant'Agata referred to on page 19. The routes described here use many of the paths on this map.

Getting about
Buses. To get the best out of the walking behind Sorrento, you will need to master the SITA bus services which radiate from the Circumvesuviana railway station. Tickets are available from the bar at the station or, if it is closed, from the bar in the square across the main road from the station. Obtain a photocopy of the current bus timetables from the official tourist office (AST). These repay careful study, as the four bus routes provide a complex pattern of service to the towns and villages where the walk segments start. For Walk segments 63, 64, 65 and 66, you may wish instead to ride to the Colli di San Pietro stop, served by the Sorrento/Amalfi service; or take the Circumvesuviana bus service direct to Fontanelle. See Timetables, beginning on page 128.

Tourist sights
The old town, west of the Piazza Tasso, is delightful to stroll around. Visit, too, the medieval cathedral, the Palazzo Correale and its museum (set in pleasant gardens with a fine view of the Bay of Naples), and the church of San Francesco, with its beautiful cloisters and gardens. All of these buildings are centrally located.

Walk planning tips
The paths immediately to the west of Sorrento offer some pleasant walks going directly from town; choose from the Walk planner. For easy walks see excursions 13 to 15 on page 23.

To walk further afield, it is best to take the bus. Choose Termini or Nerano for coastal walks (Walk segments 58 to 62). From Termini a splendid chain of paths leads back to Sorrento via Massa Lubrense and Sant'Agata (Walk segments 53, 54, 55 and 56), and these segments can be joined by bus at the intermediate points, if a shorter walk is preferred. The coastal walk from Fontanelle (Walk segment 66) is fine, as is the walk back to Sorrento from there (Walk segment 65).

If you are staying in Sorrento, consider walking in the Positano area and on Capri.

WALK SEGMENTS

48 Sorrento — Pantano

This segment takes you west out of Sorrento, avoiding main roads. It opens up other possibilities — perhaps a visit to the Villa Pollio, a Roman villa on a headland, with wide views of the Bay of Naples, or to Marina di Puolo, a pleasant small fishing village. Another scenic route is the return to Sorrento via the zigzag steps down from Crocevia, passing the fourteen Stations of the Cross. Pantano isn't even a hamlet — just the name of a junction (between the Via Pantano and the alley Via Li Simoni) from which other walk segments radiate.

48a Sorrento to Pantano

Time: 40min; *Grade:* easy, with a *height gain* of 70m/230ft

From Piazza Tasso in Sorrento, take Via San Cesareo (if Signor Tasso's marble lips could move he would say: 'from here, take the second left'). After 600m/0.35mi, at its end, turn right and then immediately left. This road leads up to the main road west out of Sorrento. • Turn right on the road and, after 50m/yds, turn left up a cobbled road opposite 'International Camping'. Go round the hairpin bend and take the path on the right, to short-cut the next hairpin. In a further 100m/yds, at a three-way fork (superb view from here of Sorrento and the Bay of Naples), take the left fork — a footpath between walls which leads up to a higher main road after 200m/yds. • Go right along main road for 100m/yds, then take a narrow unsurfaced road on the left (metal railings at the outset). Follow it round bends and through olive groves, contouring for 1km/0.6mi, until a narrow road descends on the right. Keep left for a further 100m/yds, to where the road bends right and an alley (Via Li Simoni) ascends left; this is Pantano.

48b Pantano to Sorrento

Time: 30min; *Grade:* easy

Facing the alley Via Li Simoni at Pantano, take the narrow road left. After 100m/yds, keep right and follow the road (Via Pantano), contouring round bends and through olive groves. After 1km/0.6mi, on reaching a main road, go right. After 100m/yds, turn half left down a path. Now forking downhill at each junction, you reach a lower main road. • Turn right and after only 50m/yds turn left down steps. These merge with a minor road which takes you to a cross-roads on the edge of Sorrento town centre. Go right, then immediately left; after 50m/yds you have two options to get to the town centre: go straight ahead, or else turn left, for a more scenic route with views over the coast.

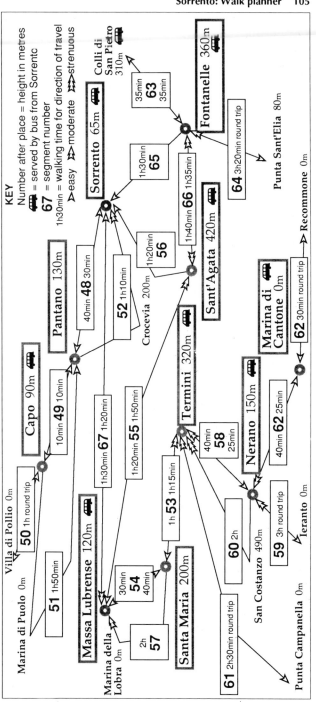

Olive groves beside our route (Walk segment 49)

49 Pantano — Capo

A short connecting segment, to/from a small village called Capo.

49a Pantano to Capo

Time: 10min; Grade: easy

With your back to the Via Li Simoni at Pantano, take the narrow road straight ahead. After 100m/yds turn right down a more important road, keeping olive groves on the right. This leads down to the main road after 500m/yds, with another minor road opposite.

49b Capo to Pantano

Time: 10min; Grade: easy, with a height gain of 40m/130ft

From Capo, take the minor road going inland from the main road. After 500m/yds turn left onto a narrow road, with an olive grove on the left. After 100m/yds you reach Patano, a junction with the alley Via Li Simoni.

50 Capo — Villa di Pollio

An 'out and back' visit to the Roman villa on the coast.

Time: 1h round trip; Grade: easy, with a height gain of 90m/300ft

From Capo, walk down the minor road going seaward (Transversa Punta Capo). This splendid cobbled road heads straight downhill to the headland (Punta del Capo) and its villa (Villa di Pollio). There is also a little inlet of the sea here which glimmers in the most beautiful of translucent colours. Return by the same route.

51 Capo — Pantano, via Marina di Puolo

Marina di Puolo is a pleasant little fishing village with bars and a restaurant. Having taken you to the village, the segment offers a way to continue on the coast road for a short way, and back on countryside paths. Or you could retrace your steps from the village to Capo.

Time: 1h50min; Grade: easy, with a height gain of 130m/430ft

From the cross-roads at Capo, walk away from Sorrento along the main road; after 200m/yds turn right under the arch of the Hotel Dania; there is a sign for Marina di Puolo here. Go left behind the hotel; this alley meets a minor road after 300m/yds; turn right and follow the road down to the fishing village of Marina di Puolo. (The next beach is private; it and the surrounding land is owned by the

Naples shipping magnate Lauro, whose large modern house on the hill beyond can be seen from Walk segments 57 and 67.) • Walk under the arch in the middle of the sea-front houses; this leads to a zigzag path behind the village. Follow it up to the main road and turn right. Continue along the main road for 800m/0.5mi, until you can turn left up Via del Generale. • Go up to the first hairpin bend (to the right). Here go straight ahead along a very narrow concrete track. After about 500m/yds, go right at a fork. The track becomes earthen, then peters out into a path. After crossing a drive, you come to a road: turn left downhill. After 100m/yds, where the road bends left in front of an olive grove, go right for 100m/yds, to Pantano, the junction of Via Pantano and Via Li Simoni.

52 Pantano to Sorrento, via Crocevia

For the price of a stiffish climb up to Priora you can return to Sorrento down dramatic zigzag steps by the church of Madonna della Dolorata and its fourteen Stations of the Cross.

Time: 1h10min; *Grade:* moderate, with a *height gain* of 130m/430ft

Take the narrow paved path (Via Li Simoni) at Pantano. Cross a concrete road after 200m/yds, continuing on the the earthen Via Paradisello. This path curves left, crosses a small stream (if the bridge is still broken, cross the stream lower down) and then curves right, becoming a narrow concrete road. You now climb steeply to a T-junction by a painting of the Madonna and Child. [Here **Walk segment 67** crosses and you can turn left for a quicker return to Sorrento or right to Massa Lubrense.] Turn right up a narrow stone-paved road; after 50m/yds turn left up another stone-paved road. • After 100m/yds you reach a main road: cross it and continue up Via Priora for 150m/yds. Now turn left up an alley that goes under an arch by a church, to a quiet road (••). Turn left and follow the road downhill for 800m/0.5mi, through the hamlet of Priora and into Crocevia. [**Walk segment 56** comes in here from the right.] • Turn left down a narrow concrete road in front of a small church. After about 400m/yds this road becomes an old stepped path that descends past the church of Madonna della Dolorata. With a Station of the Cross at each bend, you enjoy a spectacular descent to Sorrento.

53 Termini — Santa Maria

The small village of Termini sits high up near the tip of the Sorrento Peninsula. It commands splendid views of Capri, while itself being dominated by a hill on which is perched the church of San Costanzo.

The village, served by bus, is a good starting point for walks down to the coast, and for a chain of segments to take you back to Sorrento, of which this is the first. • *This segment follows ancient mule tracks through the sleepy villages of Schiazzano and Santa Maria. The tracks are now often concreted, but in many places are still paved, stepped, or even earthen. Always the views are rewarding; local agriculture and gardening can be observed first hand.* ***Photograph pages 26-27***

53a Termini to Santa Maria

Time: 1h; *Grade:* easy, with a *height gain* of 20m/65ft

Leave the main square of Termini by ascending the stone-paved road (Via delle Torre) to the left of the restaurant. Go round a bend to the left and soon take steps up to the right (on the far side of a building, the Casearina Sorrentina). • After only 100m/yds, the path leads to the crest of a hill, from where there is a fine view of Capri and the Bay of Naples — the picnic spot shown on pages 26-27. Soon an earthen track comes underfoot, then concrete. Some 800m/0.5mi after leaving Termini, you reach a wide road: turn right. • After only 100m/yds, just past a house on the left, turn left down a steep narrow track with paving in its centre. Soon this track bends right; follow it to the centre of Schiazzano. In the village, turn left to the main square (bar, pizzeria, shop). • Leave the square on the Via Santa Maria; soon it bends right and leaves the village. Notice now the coppiced sweet chestnut woodland on the right — producing poles for use in the vineyards and lemon groves. The pleasant path descends, then climbs again, up to the centre of Santa Maria. Make your way to the front of its large cream-coloured church.

53b Santa Maria to Termini

Time: 1h15min; *Grade:* moderate, with a *height gain* of 140m/460ft

From Santa Maria take the road at the left-hand side of the cream-coloured church. At the back of the church, go right on a narrow road, descending gradually to a stream, beyond which a path leads you up to the main square of Schiazzano (bar, pizzeria, shop). Take the narrow stone-paved road half right out of the square; after 100m/yds turn right up another narrow road (Via Tore di Casa). • After 500m/yds, you reach a wide road: turn right and, 100m/yds further on, go left up a concrete track. This reduces to a path as it crosses a low hill ahead (photograph pages 26-27, with a fine view of Capri and the Bay of Naples). On reaching a road, turn left to Termini.

54 Santa Maria — Massa Lubrense

This is the second segment in the chain from Termini to Sorrento. From Santa Maria you can make a pleasant detour to Annunziata by following Walk segment 57 for a short way and then retracing your steps.

54a Santa Maria to Massa Lubrense
Time: 30min; *Grade:* easy

From Santa Maria, with the front door of the church on your right, take the old paved road ahead. This soon bends left around the last building in the village and then gently descends on steps. After 300m/yds take the Via Sant'Agniello Vecchio, a narrow path forking off right between a high concrete wall on the right and the low boundary fence of a house. Some 200m/yds further on, you pass an excellent picnic spot in an olive grove, with good views over Massa Lubrense and the Bay of Naples.
• After a further 100m/yds, at a junction of paths, note the small chapel on left. This is the private chapel of the de Martino family. A very friendly woman, a last remaining member of the family, may be looking after the building. Go straight on at the junction. After a further 250m/yds, you come to another junction (the other end of the Via Sant'Agniello Vecchio; there is a sign on the wall). [If you wish to skip Massa Lubrense and continue direct to Sant'Agata on **Walk segment 55a**, turn right here.] • To get to the centre of Massa Lubrense, turn left 30m/yds further on. Then continue for another 200m/yds, gently descending to a T-junction. A right turn, followed by left, leads to the centre of Massa Lubrense (all town facilities here). The cathedral, *Municipio* and viewpoint are all further downhill.

54b Massa Lubrense to Santa Maria
Time: 40min; *Grade:* easy, with a *height gain* of 80m/260ft

Starting from the cathedral and *Municipio* in Massa Lubrense, take the wide street uphill, to the triangle in front of an imposing building. Walk along the right-hand side of the triangle and continue straight ahead up a narrow road (Via Rachione). Take first right, then the first left (Via Mortella). • After 200m/yds, at a T-junction, turn right. After 30m/yds this becomes Via Sant'Agniello Vecchio (there is a sign on the wall). [The path from Sant'Agata, **Walk segment 55**, comes in from the left here.] Continue along Via Sant'Agniello Vecchio for 250m/yds, to a junction of paths by a chapel (see notes in 54a above). Continue for another 300m/yds, through terraces, to a junction with a narrow road. Turn left up to Santa Maria.

55 Massa Lubrense — Sant'Agata
This is the third link in the chain of segments between Termini and Sorrento. (Or you could take Walk segment 67b for a direct connection to Sorrento, missing out Sant'Agata.) • *This segment passes the gates of*

the Deserto Convent. A climb to the belvedere at the top of this building is worthwhile for the far-reaching views to Capri, the peninsula and the Bay of Naples. It is open 08.30-12.30 and 14.30-16.30 (Oct-March) or 16.00-20.00 (April-Sept). Ring the bell at the main door, enter on hearing the buzzer, and a nun will lend you the key. The belvedere is entered by the adjacent door. Free, but donation requested. You pass Sant'Agata's fine old church, too, famous for its inlaid marble altars.

55a Massa Lubrense to Sant'Agata

Time: 1h50min; *Grade:* moderate, with a *height gain* of 300m/980ft

From the cathedral and *Municipio* in Massa Lubrense, follow **Walk segment 54b** (page 109) to Via Sant'Agniello Vecchio (there is a sign on the wall). Here Walk segment 54b continues ahead along Via Sant'Agniello Vecchio, but we turn left up another alley, after 100m/yds coming to a road. Cross straight over, then take Via San Francesco, an old paved path. Follow this uphill for 250m/yds, to the next road. Turn left for 50m/yds along this road and then go right up a continuation of Via San Francesco. (You could take a detour here, by going left along the road, to look at the church of San Francesco.) • After climbing the Via San Francesco (now a concrete track) for 150m/yds, turn right up Traversa San Francesco. This pleasant little path is a short-cut: it will bring you back onto the track higher up. Then continue for another 200m/yds, up to the next road (Via San Vito). Turn left and walk 400m/yds along the road to the church of San Vito (there is an *alimentari* half-way along). • Take the path (Via Tore al Deserto) at the right-hand side of the church. This paved path climbs for 250m/yds, then turns left along a drive for another 350m/yds, until a road is met at a T-junction. Turn right and follow this for 500m/yds, to a wide road at the gates of the Deserto Convent. Continue down the road past Sant'Agata's large old church and on to the centre of town

55b Sant'Agata to Massa Lubrense

Time: 1h20min; *Grade:* easy

With your back to the Hotel delle Palme in the centre of Sant'Agata, take the road to the left, passing the large old church and then walking uphill on Via Deserto. On reaching the gates of the Deserto Convent after 700m/0.4mi, take the unnamed minor road down to the right. For 500m/yds, this descends, levels out, and then descends sharply again. Some 100m/yds after the start of the second descent, turn left in front of a small walled-in olive grove. • This drive, level at first, descends for 350m/yds, to a fork in front of imposing house gates. Take the right-hand fork, a paved path down to the church of San

Vito. Walk left along the road, away from the front of the church, for 400m/yds (half-way along you pass an *alimentari*). When the road bends sharply left, take a concrete track to the right, descending steeply. • Descend for 200m/yds, to where the track bends sharp right around the corner of a house. Here follow the well-used path straight ahead — a short-cut which curves right, to rejoin the track lower down. Continue down to a road. (A detour to the right here would take you to the church of San Francesco.) Turn left along road for 50m/yds and then turn right down a path (by a phone box). Follow the path downhill for 250m/yds, to the next road. • Go straight across the road and descend an alley, now with houses on your left, for 100m/ yds. You come to a T-junction with the Via Sant'Agniello Vecchio (there is a sign on the wall on your left). [**Walk segment 54b** goes left here.] Go right for 30m/yds and then turn left. Continue for 200m/yds, gently descending to a T-junction. A right turn, followed by left, leads to the centre of Massa Lubrense (all town facilities here). The cathedral, *Municipio* and viewpoint are all further downhill.

56 Sant'Agata to Sorrento

This route provides a lovely gentle descent from Sant'Agata to Sorrento, for the most part along old mule paths and alleys, culminating with the descent of the zigzag path from the church of Santa Maria Dolorata and its fourteen Stations of the Cross. You will have splendid views over Sorrento and the Bay of Naples.

Time: 1h20min; *Grade:* easy

With your back to the Hotel delle Palme in the centre of Sant'Agata, take the road to the left for 100m/yds, then turn right (this street is identified as Via Termine a little way along). After 100m/yds go left again, down another narrow street (Via Pacliaro di Santolo). Pass beneath the main road, and continue for another 200m/yds. Then ignore a first road on the right (signed to Sorrento; an alternative route) but, after another 30m/yds, take the second right (at a T-junction). • This road descends, curves left and levels out. Where it descends sharp right continue straight ahead on a narrow road, descending gently. When the road ends after 250m/yds, go straight ahead on a path signposted in English 'Sorrento, for foot passengers'. It climbs gently for 150m/yds, to a T-junction, where you turn right down an old paved path. Follow this for about 250m/yds, then continue on a narrow road for another 250m/yds, to an oblique T-junction with a wider road. Turn right downhill for 50m/yds, to a small church.

On the path between Santa Maria and Annunziata, with Capri in the distance (Walk segment 57).

You are now in Crocevia. From here follow the final part of **Walk segment 52** to Sorrento.

57 Santa Maria — Marina della Lobra — Massa Lubrense

With its wide views and elegant old buildings along the way, this is an exceptionally fine segment. Only the final ascent to Massa Lubrense disappoints slightly, the paths then being enclosed by walls. **Photograph above and page 12**

Time: 2h; *Grade:* moderate, with a *height gain* of 120m/390ft

With your back to the church in Santa Maria, go left (Via Annunziata). After 200m/yds, take the narrow road half right, a short-cut to the next road. Some 100m/yds along this road, look for an alley going right (Salita Castello), up to the castle (which always seems to be closed for repairs) and down to the main square in Annunziata with its large church (also a ➥). • Just beyond the square there is a lovely little park with seats and a fine view out to Capri. Continue past the park, descending the road to where it ends by an old house, the Villa Rossi. From here, in 1808, the King of Naples directed the siege of the English who were then occupying Capri, and it was in this house that their surrender was signed, by Hudson Lowe. • Continue down the steps ahead through delightful olive groves, keeping right at a junction of minor roads. On reaching the main road, turn right for 50m/yds, to the church of San Liberatore, which presents fine views down to Marina della Lobra. From the church piazza, take the level path (Via San Liberatore), to contour behind the fishing village for 800m/0.5mi, to a T-junction with a narrow stone-paved road. • From here you should turn left to go down to Marina della Lobra (15min return; bars overlooking the harbour; restaurant open in summer). Retrace your steps and continue uphill to the next junction. Turn left on Via Pipiano. After 100m/yds continue up Via del Canneto; soon steps take you up to a road. Take more steps on the far side and, after 40m/yds, turn left on Via Sirignano. Some 150m/yds along, an old (1728) building faces you; turn right here, up a narrow passage. After 100m/yds turn right up Via Pennino to the main street in Massa Lubrense.

58 Termini — Nerano

This is the first part of a super descent to the clear waters of Ieranto, a World Wild Life preservation area. You could skip this segment by staying on the bus and starting from the next village, Nerano. Having enjoyed a visit to Ieranto (Walk segment 59) and returned to Nerano (or perhaps on another day), you could take a rather steep, but very rewarding return route to Termini (Walk segment 60); it ascends the nearby twin mountain peaks of San Costanzo. • If, instead of taking these rather rough paths, you prefer an easy route, you can walk down a delightful path from Nerano to the fleshpots and beach of Marina di Cantone, with an optional extension to Recommone (Walk segment 62).

58a Termini to Nerano

Time: 25min; *Grade:* easy

With your back to the church in Termini, turn left and, after 50m/yds, at the bend, *start* to turn right on Via Campanella. Just under the road name, descend steps (Via Grottone). These lead into a path and then a narrow concrete road. • Follow it downhill for 600m/0.35mi, to a T-junction with another narrow concrete road: turn right. The road narrows to a stepped alley and descends to the road in the centre of Nerano (church, bar and shop).

58b Nerano to Termini

Time: 40min; *Grade:* moderate, with a *height gain* of 170m/560ft

Opposite the church in Nerano, climb the steps (Via Fontana di Nerano). After 100m/yds, turn left up steps through an arch under a house (Via Grottone). After another 300m/yds (after the path has widened into a minor road), turn left up a narrower concrete road. After a further 600m/0.35mi uphill you reach Termini.

59 Nerano — Ieranto

This 'out and back' walk takes you down to the unspoilt rocky peninsula and delightful small bathing beach of Ieranto, with splendid views along the coast and to Capri. The waters are a World Wild Life site on account of their clarity and abundance of sea life. The timing makes a one hour allowance for exploring, picnicking and bathing — you could easily justify more. Although the track is excellent, the final part and the terrain on the peninsula is rough and rocky — possibly best done in boots.

Time: 3h round trip; *Grade:* moderate, with a *height gain* of 170m/560ft

With your back to the church in Nerano, turn left along

the road (Via Amerigo Vespucci) for 50m/yds. Take the path leading off right (Via Ieranto). [After 100m/yds, note the red/white waymarks on the zigzag path going up to the right; **Walk segment 60**] • Continue straight ahead along the track; it ascends gradually for about 1km/0.6mi, contours a steep slope high above the sea, and passes a house (Villa Rosa). Then the track narrows and descends for 300m/yds between low walls, to another house on the left. Just beyond this the full view of the peninsula opens out. • Here the path splits; either go straight ahead down a long flight of concrete steps to the bathing beach, or fork left and descend to a gate in the rather decrepit fence bounding the FAI (*Fondazione Ambiente Italiano*) reserve. Ignore the 'privato' sign and walk past the smallholding; the farmer doesn't mind people passing through his property — especially if you are courteous enough to pass the time of day with him in this lonely place. From the smallholding the path contours and then descends steeply through olive groves to the beach. Consider exploring the two peaks of the peninsula and the ruined watch-tower.
• Allow an hour for the return to Nerano.

60 Nerano to Termini, via San Costanzo

The views from the twin peaks of San Costanzo are outstanding. Before you, the spine of the mountainous Sorrento Peninsula recedes into the distance, with the Bay of Naples laid out to the left. Out in a glittering sea, Capri rises starkly. You can walk straight up the military road from Termini, but this segment, while rather strenuous, is more interesting.
Photograph opposite

Time: 2h; *Grade:* strenuous, with a *height gain* of 360m/1180ft

With your back to the church in Nerano, turn left along the road (Via Amerigo Vespucci) for 50m/yds, then take the path to the right (Via Ieranto). After 100m/yds of gentle ascent, by low steel gates, turn right up a zigzag path, initially on concrete steps. From here the red/white CAI marks will be your guide to the top of the mountain. • The path zigzags steeply up through wood, then open, rough terrain, until the gradient relents at a smallholding. Take the well-trodden path that hugs the seaward side of the smallholding. At first the path contours, and you approach the near corner of a first wood on your left. Here the path ascends half right — towards the point where the edge of another wood ahead meets the crest of the ridge. (There is a well-trodden path all the way, but keeping to it in the tussocky grass requires vigilance.) • Once on the crest of the ridge, turn right up an excellent old track to the chapel on the eastern summit. From here it is worth walking back along the crest, to a road up to the gates of a military compound on the western summit, for splendid views of Capri. • To return to Termini, descend the old track from the chapel — you can join it a short way down the access road.

61 Termini — Punta Campanella

From Termini an excellent, well-graded track leads down to the light-house that marks the extreme tip of the Sorrento Peninsula. On the way you have fine views of Capri, just a few kilometres out to sea.

Time: 2h30min round trip; *Grade:* moderate, with a *height gain of 320m/1050ft*

With your back to the church in Termini, turn left; after 50m/yds, at the bend, turn right down Via Campanella. After 150m/yds, follow the road to the right. This road descends gradually all the way to the lighthouse, with the hillside up to your left. Return the same way.

62 Nerano — Marina di Cantone — Recommone

A delightful, easy path leads from Nerano down past small houses and gardens with snatches of fine views as you go. From Marina di Cantone an easy coastal path takes you round the headland to Recommone, where there is a restaurant and bar (open only in summer). There are beaches at both places, the one at Marina di Cantone being especially well sited. The bars and restaurants in Marina di Cantone are open all year round; it's one of the places where the citizens of Sorrento go to

The delightful path from Nerano down to Marina di Cantone (Tour 1, Excursion 13, Walk segment 62). Above broods Monte San Costanzo, with its hilltop chapel (Tour 1 and Walk segment 60).

eat in the summer, when their own town is crowded out with visitors. Look for the church of San Antonio at the left-hand end of the beach.
Photograph page 115

62a Nerano to Marina di Cantone
Time: 25min plus 30min round trip to Recommone; *Grade:* easy

From Nerano take the passage down to the right of the church (Via Cantone). Follow this all the way down to Marina di Cantone (you cross the main road twice). The path round the headland to Recommone starts at the left-hand side of the beach, to the left of the last restaurant.

62b Marina di Cantone to Nerano
Time: 40min; *Grade:* moderate, with a *height gain* of 150m/500ft

From Marina di Cantone, go up the left-hand side of the large narrow car park (Largo Argentina). This path leads up to the church in Nerano, twice crossing the main road.

63 Colli di San Pietro — Fontanelle

Colli di San Pietro is the name of the bus stop at the highest point on the Sorrento/Positano road. From here you can easily take this segment to the village of Fontanelle, then choose between a splendid out-and-back coastal walk on an excellent path (Walk segment 64), a fine coastal walk to Sant'Agata (Walk segment 66), or the return on foot down to Sorrento (Walk segment 65). (Note that if you are coming from Sorrento, you can take the Circumvesuviana bus straight to Fontanelle.)

63a Colli di San Pietro to Fontanelle
Time: 35min; *Grade:* easy, with a *height gain* of 70m/230ft

At the Colli di San Pietro, with your back to the gate posts with the name 'Belvedere Massa', walk left along the road towards Sant'Agata for 600m/0.35mi, to a sharp bend to the left. Here take the minor road (Via Bosco) straight ahead; it narrows into a path, crosses a small hill and, after 700m/0.4mi, comes to a T-junction: turn left. Cross the road to ascend a cobbled street, passing a large church on the left. You meet the main road again after 500m/yds, at a cross-roads by a bar and shop. This is Fontanelle.

63b Fontanelle to Colli di San Pietro
Time: 35min; *Grade:* easy, with a *height gain* of 40m/130ft

From the shop at the cross-roads in Fontanelle, turn left on the main road; 50m/yds along, fork right on a minor street. After 500m/yds you pass a large church on the right and rejoin the main road. Cross straight over, then immediately turn right on a path. It takes you over a small hill, and you regain the road after 700m/0.4mi. Continue ahead on this road for 600m/0.35mi, to meet the Sorrento/Positano road at a cross-roads, the Colli di San Pietro.

64 Fontanelle — Punta Sant'Elia

Years ago farmers built a small settlement to scratch a living from the slopes of Punta Sant'Elia, a remote headland below Fontanelle, justifying the construction of an excellent mule track that descends by wild cliffs and across shrub-covered slopes. A few buildings and some fruit trees remain to testify to the former activity.

Time: 3h20min round trip; *Grade:* moderate, with a *height gain* of 340m/1120ft

From the shop at the cross-roads in Fontanelle, turn right along the main road for 50m/yds, and then turn left down a side-road (Via Belvedere). Follow it gradually downhill, to the belvedere car park. The coastal path leaves from here (signposted 'Via S Elia') and descends for 1.5km/1mi, often on steps, to two abandoned buildings. From here you can continue a short distance further on a level path, to a good view and picnic spot. Return the same way.

65 Fontanelle to Sorrento

The hillsides behind Sorrento have seen quite a lot of new house building, but it is still possible to follow old tracks. On the heights you enjoy expansive views of the Bay of Naples and Sorrento's setting; lower down you wend your way through the interesting older outskirts of the town. An attractive route and, of course, downhill most of the way.

Time: 1h30min; *Grade:* easy, with a *height gain* of 60m/200ft

With your back to the bar in Fontanelle, turn left onto a narrow level road that starts by contouring the hillside. Soon fork left on Via Rocca; it climbs gradually, giving magnificent views to the right. On reaching its highest point, the road bends left and starts descending the opposite slope — a steep concrete track between gardens, with views down to Sorrento. After 600m/0.35mi of descent, the road bends right and contours for 300m/yds, until it again reaches the crest of the ridge, offering more views of the Bay of Naples. • Turn left downhill. After 450m/yds, a surfaced road is reached (by a barrier). Turn right and follow this road round a curve to the left (viewpoint); 400m/yds further on there is a second viewpoint (with car park). Just before this, take the narrow road down to the right. Just round the first bend, turn left, straight down the hillside, on a delightful stone-paved path through an olive grove. Eventually you meet a lower, narrow road (Via Casola) at a T-junction: turn left. • Follow this road past Sorrento cemetery; after 600m/0.35mi, at a T-junction with a main road, turn right. Go round the bend, then turn left on a cobbled road. This road comes out on the Via degli Aranci, opposite the road down to Sorrento railway station.

66 Fontanelle — Sant'Agata

This CAI route provides a good path from Fontanelle to a splendid stretch of coastline, high above the sea and with excellent views to Positano

Asphodels brighten walks throughout the region. These were seen in March on Walk segment 66, near the grassy promontory on the coast. The meadows were carpeted with anemones then.

and Capri. Having reached a superb coastal viewpoint, where the CAI path descends steeply to continue along the coast, we cut inland, to traverse a pine-covered hill, before descending to Sant'Agata. The route is equally fine in the opposite direction. **Photographs above and pages 100-101**

66a Fontanelle to Sant'Agata
Time: 1h40min; *Grade:* moderate, with a *height gain* of 200m/660ft
From Fontanelle climb the minor road (Via Pietre Piana) between the bar and the shop. Go beyond the houses, keeping straight ahead, to the main road. Cross it and take a path on the far side, to rejoin the main road higher up. Go left for 200m/yds, to a sharp right-hand bend. Here take the path that ascends gently and then contours towards the coast, through light woodland. At a fork 50m/yds along, keep left. After a further 100m/yds, look for a small tree on the right with red/white CAI waymarks. Just 20m/yds beyond this, take the narrow well-trodden path climbing up to the right through woodland. Once out of the wood, more red/white waymarks guide you. The path levels out high above the coast. After contouring for 300m/yds, you come to a grassy promontory which provides a grandstand view of the coast — a superb picnic spot. We leave the CAI waymarks here. • Look inland for an old red-roofed farm building 150m/yds away, a little lower down, and in light woodland. Make for this by

minor tracks, descending initially. Once there, turn right on an earthen path that starts on a low embankment. The path leads up to the corner of a fence which you follow, keeping it to your right. Curving in a wide sweep to the left, some 500m/yds from the building you come to a track, and then a surfaced road. • After another 150m/yds, a pine wood opens up on the right. Either continue on the road (views) or take the path in the wood along the crest of the hill (shade); this path runs parallel with the road and rejoins it after 1km/0.6mi. Beyond the wood the road descends to a restaurant on the left (only open in summer) and a T-junction. Turn left and after 100m/yds, at a fork, turn right. This narrow road descends in wide bends between houses for 1km/0.6mi (fine views) to a wider road. Turn right for 300m/yds, to a T-junction by the houses of Sant'Agata. Turn left to the town centre.

66b Sant'Agata to Fontanelle
Time: 1h35min; *Grade:* moderate, with a *height gain* of 140m/460ft

With your back to the Hotel delle Palme in Sant'Agata, take the road straight ahead. After 150m/yds turn right (Via Pontone). In a further 300m/yds turn left on a narrow road (by a telephone kiosk). The road curves between houses and rises steadily for 1km/0.6mi, to a junction with another minor road. Turn left, then immediately curve right past a restaurant on the right (open only in summer). After 200m/yds a path leads into a pine wood on the left. Either continue on the road (views) or take the woodland path along the crest of the hill (shade); it rejoins the road after 1km/0.6mi. • Some 150m/yds past the wood, the road narrows to a track, then (by a house) an earthen path. For 500m/yds it sweeps to the right, descending gently, skirting a fence on the left. Where the fence ends, continue ahead for 100m/yds, to an old farm building with red-tiled roof. From its left-hand wall, follow the small level path running parallel with the coast for 150m/yds, until you clear the wood; then ascend to a grassy promontory, from where there is a fine view of the coast (superb picnic spot). • Turn left on a level path, walking parallel with the coast, but high above it. At the end of the wall on the left, pick up a well-trodden path marked at intervals with red/white CAI waymarks. Follow it, parallel with the coast, for 300m/yds; then curve inland, gradually descending. Beyond woodland, you meet the main road: turn right. After 200m/yds, turn right again, down a path. On meeting the road again, cross it and walk straight down a minor road to Fontanelle cross-roads (shop, bar).

67 Sorrento — Massa Lubrense

Massa Lubrense and Sorrento lie only 4km apart so, instead of going by bus, why not take this walk amid olive groves and gardens?

67a Sorrento to Massa Lubrense

Time: 1h30min; *Grade:* moderate, with a *height gain* of 160m/530ft

From Sorrento, follow **Walk segment 48a** (page 104) up the cobbled road opposite 'International Camping'. Keep ahead round all hairpin bends (three short-cut paths), until the road climbs straight away from Sorrento. After 150m/yds the road turns left; here go straight ahead on a path (Via Priora) to the main road. Cross it and climb Via Priora. After 200m/yds, at a fork with a Madonna and Child painting, go left uphill. [**Walk segment 52** comes up from the right here and goes left at the next turning.]
• Now climbing more gently continue straight ahead for another 700m/0.4mi. From the top of the hill, continue ahead for 400m/yds, to a cross-roads. Go straight over to join Via Bagnulo. After 350m/yds, after walking under an arch beneath a white house, take the first right. This road descends round two bends, after 150m/yds reaching a T-junction: turn left. After 150m/yds take the first right, then continue straight ahead to the centre of Massa Lubrense.

67b Massa Lubrense to Sorrento

Time: 1h20min; *Grade:* easy, with a *height gain* of 110m/360ft

From Massa Lubrense, follow **Walk segment 54b** (page 109) to Via Rachione. Keep up this road for 250m/yds. On meeting a road, cross it and climb Via Bagnulo. At a T-junction turn left. After 150m/yds (where the way ahead is an earthen path), follow the road up to the right, rounding two bends. At a T-junction turn left. • After 350m/yds, at a cross-roads, go ahead on Via Monte Corbo. After another 400m/yds of gentle climbing, you reach the top of the hill; descend for 700m/0.4mi, to a turning left, where there is a painting of the Madonna and Child. [**Walk segment 52** comes up from the left here and goes right at the previous turning.] Keep right here, descending 200m/yds to a hairpin bend on the main road. Cross straight over onto a path and continue downhill, to join Via Capodimonte. Shortly this road descends in a series of hairpin bends to the main road (short-cut paths, and superb views of Sorrento and the Bay of Naples). • Turn right and after only 50m/yds turn left down steps. These widen out into a minor road. At a cross-roads on the edge of Sorrento, go right, then immediately left; after 50m/yds, you have two options to reach the town centre: go straight ahead, or turn left for a more scenic route, with views over the coast.

❀ Capri

Capri lies six kilometres out to sea, an elongated rocky protuberance 7km long and 3km across at its widest point. It is ringed by high limestone cliffs much of the way round, rising to 589m/1900ft at its highest point, Monte Solaro. Above the cliffs the terrain, although hilly, is gentle enough to allow habitation and gardening on the fertile soil. The main town of Capri occupies the spine of the eastern half of the island, spilling down the slopes north and south to the harbours of Marina Grande and Marina Piccola. A cliff crosses the island, isolating the western half, occupied by the higher town of Anacapri (a much quieter place than its brasher neighbour). A road has been cut into the cliff-face to connect the two towns, and a funicular railway will whisk you up from the Marina Grande to Capri town.

In summer an endless stream of large modern ferries disgorges so many day visitors onto the Marina Grande that congestion hinders people getting to the funicular and, when they do finally succeed, they fill to overflowing the squares of the main town up on its hilltop. Then, while browsing in the boutiques, they complain of the crush. But here, as anywhere else, you can get away from the crowds in no time at all … and walk through the tranquil flower-bedecked world that has enticed so many of the rich and famous to live here. Narrow roads swathed in bougainvillaea and redolent of jasmine, and used only by pedestrians and the occasional electric trolley, lead past fine houses with ornamental and kitchen gardens to the island's sensational coastline. A visit to this magical place should figure in every itinerary, best of all in winter.

See notes on page 19 about maps and a walking guide.

Getting about
The *funicular* will take you efficiently in just a few minutes from the Marina Grande up to the main town. *Buses* go from both the Marina Grande and Capri town along the switchback road to Anacapri, higher up to the west and, from there, a bus runs down to the Blue Grotto (Grotta Azzura). From Anacapri you can take the *chair lift* (May to October only) to the summit of Monte Solaro (Excursion 17; photograph page 23).

Left: The piazza in front of San Michele in Anacapri (Excursion 17, Walk segment 72). Right: Greenery sprouts from the Roman brickwork of Tiberius' villa (Villa Jovis, Excursion 16, Walk segment 68)

Tourist sights

Apart from Villa Jovis (see Walk segment 68), in Capri you could visit the restored monastery of Certosa, or the Gardens of Augusto, for their view. In Anacapri there is the Villa San Michele, once home to the Swedish writer Axel Munthe, built around the remains of a Roman villa.

Walk planning tips

The segments 68, 69 and 70 together offer a full day's walking, at a reasonably gentle pace to allow time for sight-seeing. They effectively cover the eastern end of the island, the most popular part. Views change rapidly and interest is always there. If you wish to do just one or two of these, Walk segments 69 and 70 probably provide more variety than 68. Walk segment 73 takes you easily back down to the harbour at the end of the day. Entrance to the Villa Jovis is free if you hail from the EU and are over 60 or under 18 — take your passport as proof.

Walk segments 72 and 73 are easy strolls on the western half of the island, visiting a finely-sited Roman villa and taking in some spectacular coastal scenery. Both start in Anacapri which is itself delightful to explore.

WALK SEGMENTS

68 Capri — Villa Jovis

This segment takes you up to the superbly-situated Roman villa at the top of the island's easternmost peak; the site itself is well worth the time and cost of entrance.

Time: 1h15min round trip; *Grade:* easy, with a *height gain* of 200m/660ft

From the funicular in Capri, turn left around the main tower, into a little square. Go through the small arch in the far left-hand side, on Via Longano (you could buy your picnic here). After 100m/yds bend right, into Via Sopramonte. Follow this for 400m/yds, to a cross-roads,

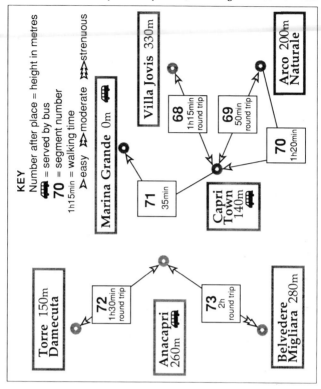

KEY
🚌 = served by bus
Number after place = height in metres
70 = segment number
1h15min = walking time
➢easy ➢➢moderate ➢➢➢strenuous

where the Villa Jovis signposted to the left and the Arco Naturale straight on. Go left. • This path climbs gently but steadily for 1.5km/1mi to the Villa Jovis (↦ on the left after 40m/yds and another at public toilets half-way along; restaurant/bar two-thirds of the way up). Return same way to the cross-roads.

69 Capri — Arco Naturale

This large natural arch is set in a fine piece of pine-clad cliff scenery, with an azure sea far below. The path takes you there easily. There are some seats there for your picnic, or a well-situated bar/restaurant lies on the path 5min before the arch. **Photograph page 126**

Time: 50min round trip; *Grade:* easy, with a *height gain* of 100m/330ft
Follow **Walk segment 68** (opposite) to the cross-roads, then go straight ahead (Via Matermania; signposted 'Arco Naturale'). Return the same way or by Walk segment 70.

70 Arco Naturale to Capri via the coast path

A very well built path takes you around the rugged southeastern cliffs, with an easy return to town along a delightfully verdant alley. On the way you encounter various points of interest — the Grotta di

The Villa Malaparte, a fururistic house lying low on a headland, built for writer Curzio Malaparte in 1938 by the Trentino architect Libera (Walk segment 70).

Matermania, a large cave with Roman remains; the Villa Malaparte (shown above); and the famous Faraglione islands (photograph page 23), three limestone fangs rising from a blue sea — Capri's trademark when viewed from along the Amalfi Coast. **Photograph above**

Time: 1h20min; *Grade:* easy, with a *height gain* of 50m/160ft

From the restaurant near the Arco Naturale, descend the steep steps signposted 'Grotta Matermania'. This path levels out at the cave and then leads you easily by the landmarks mentioned above. Finally, on reaching the narrow town road (Via Tragara), go ahead for 800m/ 0.5mi, to a cross-roads by a small square (Li Campi). Go right for 100m/yds, past boutiques, to the main square.

71 Capri — Marina Grande
This segment provides a more gentle descent to the harbour than does the direct route.

Time: 35min; *Grade:* easy

Beside the tower near the funicular in Capri descend a short flight of steps. The passage underneath the tower is the direct route to the harbour, but turn left, past a public toilet. After 100m/yds fork left and climb gently for a short time, then descend. At the next lowest point in the path, turn right down into Traversa Lo Palazzo. • After 100m/yds cross the road and continue down Via Marucella. During the next 500m/yds, ignore two signs to the right 'Al Porto Marina Grande'; continue straight ahead. Just past the Ristorante San Costanzo, you have a fine view of the 'Scale Fenicia' (Phoenician Steps) zigzagging up the cliff. Before the motor road was built in 1877, these were the only way up to Anacapri; sadly, they are now crumbled and out of use. At an oblique T-junction, turn sharp right down to the main road, then turn left to the harbour.

72 Anacapri — Torre Damecuta

This 'out and back' route takes you through the delightful town of Anacapri, amongst its outlying houses and gardens, and finally to a super viewpoint with a medieval tower and extensive Roman remains. Return by the same route or pick up one of the buses returning from the Grotta Azzurra. **Photographs pages 4-5, 122**

Time: 1h30min round trip; *Grade:* easy, with a *height gain* of 140m/ 460ft (on the return)

From the Piazza Vittoria in Anacapri (the second bus stop on reaching the town), take the path that descends gently between shops. After 200m/yds pass the Casa Rossa on the right, built around an Aragonese tower by an American colonel in 1876; note the ornate doorway. In a further 100m/yds turn right on Via San Nicola (where a map of the western half of the island is depicted in ceramic tiles). Go past the church of San Michele on the left, beyond which the path bends left into a narrow passage. You pass to the left of the residence of a former parliamentary deputy; Giuseppe Orlandi, responsible for the construction of the motor road to Anacapri in 1877. • The passage joins a wider alley, with bougainvillaea-clad palms in its centre. This bends to the right. Soon fork right, then turn left at a T-junction, to join a minor motor road. At this point the roads are named, and you walk from Via Boffe to Via la Vigna. After 150m/yds turn left into Traversa la Vigna. This descends gradually, becomes wider and opens up views of Ischia on the skyline. After 350m/yds on the *traversa,* where the path bends to the right, descend steps straight ahead. • After 200m/yds there are turnings off to the left and right; keep ahead. The way narrows into a pedestrian path beyond a barrier. After 250m/yds the path ends; turn left on Traversa Damecuta. On reaching a main road after 100m/yds, turn right. This main road turns left immediately: go straight ahead (Via Amadeo Mauri). This leads after 400m/yds along a splendid balcony path, to the Torre Damecuta site. • If the site is locked, with care you can get over the fence easily, just as the locals do. Inside there are Roman and medieval remains, information boards in English, and pine trees for a shady picnic. To return, go back to the main road and there either pick up a bus coming up from the Blue Grotto (pay on board) or walk back the same way — take the first left, the first right, and then the upward choice at all junctions.

Looking through the Arco Naturale to the coast far below (Excursion 16, Walk segment 69)

73 Anacapri — Belvedere Migliara

This segment visits the southwest of the island, with views to the lighthouse, then follows the coast path up to a spectacular viewpoint looking past towering cliffs to the Faraglione Islands. On the way to the belvedere we go through the little village of Caprile; coming back (by a different route) we follow a minor road with extensive views. Long trousers are advisable; the coast path is overgrown. (The viewpoint may also be reached directly from the Piazza Vittoria: take Via Caposcuro by the chairlift station; after 400m/yds fork left, then go straight ahead.)

Time: 2h round trip; *Grade;* moderate, with a *height gain* of 190m/620ft

From the Piazza Vittoria in Anacapri, take the path that descends gently between shops. After 400m/yds you come to a T-junction, where the white church of Santa Sofia is on the right. Turn left. Another delightful alley takes you to a minor motor road. Cross and continue ahead on Via Caprile for 200m/yds, to the piazza in Caprile (the terminus for buses coming from Capri). • Descend the steps (Via Falligara). After 100m/yds, at a fork, keep left downhill. At a T-junction turn left along Via Faro. After 300m/yds, at a junction by a glass-cased Madonna, turn right and then left. In a further 150m/yds you reach a motor road: go right but, after 50m/yds, turn left on a narrow road. You pass the entrance (on your right) to the medieval Torre di Materita, owned by the Munthe family (of the Villa San Michele in Anacapri) and not open to the public. The path skirts the wall (on your right) of the estate, descending, then climbing gradually. After 1km/0.6mi you reach the gate of the Torre Guardia, a medieval fortification reconstructed by the English during their occupation of the island in 1807. • Go left, then immediately right on a narrow footpath (beside the end wall of the *torre* grounds). This path now follows the coast for about 600m/0.35mi, climbing through bushes. The well-trodden path is always easy to find, but progress is slow because it is overgrown, often rocky underfoot, and uphill. The views along the cliffs and back down to the Punta Carena lighthouse are stunning. • Just when you begin to think the path will never end, you reach a narrow paved road at a viewpoint with seats. But continue by path, up to a more spectacular viewpoint about 100m/yds further up the coast (more seats, and views out to the Faraglione Islands). • To return to Anacapri, go back to the first viewpoint and follow the narrow paved road for 2km/1.2mi to the Piazza Vittoria. The way is level, and you enjoy fine views of the island and across the bay to Ischia as you go. There is a restaurant (open only in summer) not far past the viewpoint.

BUS TIMETABLES

Below are the bus stops shown in the walk planners, followed by the numbers of the relevant *timetables* we list below. All services are operated by the sɪᴛᴀ bus company, unless otherwise stated. See information about bus travel on pages 8-9 and price guide on page 133. *You should confirm these times locally before travelling.*

Agerola 6
Amalfi 1, 2, 3, 4, 6
Anacapri 12
Atrani 1, 3
Bomerano 6
Capitignano 5
Capo 8, 9
Colli di San Pietro 2
Conca dei Marini 2
Corsano 5
Erchie 1

Fontanelle 11
Furore 2
Grotta Azzurra 12
Herculaneum 13
Maiori 1, 5
Marina di Cantone 9, 10
Marina Grande 12
Massa Lubrense 8, 9
Minori 1

Monte Pertuso 7
Nastro Azzurro 10
Nerano 9, 10
Pogerola 4
Polvica 5
Positano 2, 7
Praiano 2
Ravello 3
Salerno 1
San Lazzaro 6
Sant'Agata 8, 10, 11

Santa Maria de Olearia 1
Scala 3
Sorrento 2, 8, 9, 10, 11
Termini 9, 10
Titigliano 8
Tramonti 5
Vesuvius 13
Vèttica Maggiore 2

1 Amalfi — Salerno, via Minori and Maiori

Salerno	Maiori	Minori	Amalfi	Amalfi	Minori	Maiori	Salerno
06.45*	07.35*	07.40*	07.55*	06.00	06.15	06.20	07.10
07.30	08.20	08.25	08.40	06.30*	06.45*	06.50*	07.40*
08.00*	08.50*	08.55*	09.10*	07.05*	07.20*	07.25*	08.15*
09.00	09.50	09.55	10.10	07.10	07.25	07.30	08.20
09.50	10.40	10.45	11.00	08.05*	08.20*	08.25*	09.15*
10.30*	11.20*	11.25*	11.40*	08.30	08.45	08.50	09.40
11.30	12.20	12.25	12.40	09.00*	09.15*	09.20*	10.10*
12.00*	12.50*	12.55*	13.10*	10.00	10.15	10.20	11.10
12.45	13.35	13.40	13.55	11.00	11.15	11.20	12.10
13.20*	14.10*	14.15*	14.30*	12.10	12.25	12.30	13.20
14.00	14.50	14.55	15.10	13.15*	13.30*	13.35*	14.25*
14.30*	15.20*	15.25*	15.40*	14.10	14.25	14.30	15.20
15.30	16.20	16.25	16.40	15.15	15.30	15.35	16.25
16.30	17.20	17.25	17.40	16.00	16.15	16.20	17.10
17.00*	17.50*	17.55*	18.10*	17.00*	17.15*	17.20*	18.10*
17.30	18.20	18.25	18.40	18.00	18.15	18.20	19.10
18.30*	19.20*	19.25*	19.40*	19.00	19.15	19.20	20.10
19.30	20.20	20.25	20.40	19.30*	19.45*	19.50*	20.40*
20.30	21.20	21.25	21.40	20.00*	20.15*	20.20*	20.10*
21.30*	22.20*	22.25*	22.40*	21.00	21.15	21.20	22.10

*Not on Sundays and holidays. *Note:* Atrani lies between Amalfi and Minori; Santa Maria de Olearia and Erchie lie between Maiori and Salerno.

2 Sorrento — Amalfi, via Positano and Praiano

Sorrento	Positano	Praiano	Amalfi	Amalfi	Praiano	Positano	Sorrento
06.35*	07.10*	07.35*	08.00*	07.10*	07.35*	08.00*	08.45*
08.25	09.00	09.25	09.50	08.05	08.30	08.55	09.40
09.15*	09.50*	10.15*	10.40*	09.30	09.55	10.20	11.05
10.05	10.40	11.05	11.30	10.45	11.10	11.35	12.20
11.25	12.00	12.25	12.50	12.10*	12.35*	13.00*	13.45*
12.35	13.10	13.35	14.00*	13.30*	13.55*	14.20*	15.05*
14.05	14.40	15.05	15.30	14.30	14.55	15.20	16.05
15.15*	15.50*	16.15*	16.40*	16.00*	16.25*	16.50*	17.35*
16.25	17.00	17.25	17.50	17.00	17.25	17.50	18.35
18.15*	18.50*	19.15*	19.40*	18.10*	18.35*	19.00*	19.45*
19.05	19.40	20.05	20.30	19.00**	19.25**	19.50**	20.35**
20.05*	20.40*	21.05*	21.30*	20.00*	20.25*	20.50*	21.35*
21.45*	22.30*	22.55*	23.20*	21.40*	22.05*	22.30*	23.15*

*Not Sundays/holidays. *Note:* Colli di San Pietro lies between Sorrento and Positano; Vèttica Maggiore between Positano and Praiano; Conca and Furore between Praiano and Amalfi.

3 Amalfi — Ravello — Amalfi, via Scala

Amalfi	Scala	Ravello	Scala	Amalfi
	06.00*	06.05*		06.30*
	06.15**	06.20**		06.45**
07.00*	07.25*	07.30*		08.00*
08.00		08.25	08.30	09.00
09.00*	09.25*	09.30*		10.00*
10.00		10.25	10.30	11.00
11.00		11.25	11.30	12.00
12.00	12.25	12.30		13.00
13.00		13.25	13.30	14.00
14.10*		14.35*	14.40*	15.10*
15.30	15.55	16.00		16.30
16.30		16.55	17.00	17.30
17.30		17.55	18.00	18.30
18.50	19.15	19.20		19.50
20.00*		20.25*	20.30*	21.00*
20.30*		20.55*	21.00*	21.30*
21.00		21.25	21.30	22.00
22.00*		22.25*	22.30*	

*Not on Sundays and holidays   *Note:* Atrani lies between Amalfi and Scala/Ravello
**Sundays and holidays only

4 Amalfi — Pogerola — Amalfi (for Tramonti)

Amalfi	Pogerola	Amalfi	Amalfi	Pogerola	Amalfi
	05.55	06.15	15.10*	15.30*	15.50*
06.20*	06.40*	07.00*	16.00	16.20	16.40
07.20*	07.20*	08.00*	16.50	17.10	17.30
08.10	08.30	08.50	17.30*	17.50*	18.10*
09.00	09.20	09.40	18.20	18.40	17.00
10.00	10.20	10.40	19.20	19.40	20.00
10.40*	11.00*	11.20*	20.00	20.20	20.40
11.30	11.50	12.10	21.00	21.20	21.40
12.20	12.40	13.00	21.50	22.10	22.30
13.15	13.35	13.55	22.40	23.00	23.20
* 14.10*	14.30*	14.50*			

Not on Sundays and holidays

5 Maiori — Polvica — Capitignano (for Tramonti)

Maiori	Bivio Polvica	Polvica	Capitig- nano	Capitig- nano	Polvica	Bivio Polvica	Maiori
06.35*	06.50*‡	07.05*	07.15*	06.35	06.50§		07.15
07.15*		07.35*	07.45*	07.45*	07.55*	08.00*‡	08.15*
08.20*	08.35*‡	08.50*	09.00*	09.15*	09.35*§		09.55*
10.00*		10.20*§	10.40*	10.45*	10.55*	11.00*‡	11.15*
10.45**		11.05**	11.15**	11.15**	11.25**		11.45**
10.45*	11.00*‡	11.05*	11.15*	13.00*	13.10*		13.30*
11.30*	11.45*‡	11.50*§	12.10*	14.25*	14.35*	14.50*‡	15.05*
11.55**		12.15**§	12.35**	15.45*	16.05*§		16.25*
13.35*	13.50*‡	13.55*§	14.15*	17.20*	17.30*	17.40*‡	17.55*
15.15*	15.30*‡	15.35*	15.45*	18.00*	18.10*		18.30*
16.30*		16.50*	17.00*				
17.20*	17.35*‡	17.40*§	18.00*				
18.30*		18.50*	19.00*				
19.20*	19.35*‡	19.40*§	20.00*				

*Not on Sundays and holidays
**Sundays and holidays only

Note: Bivio = turn-off to
‡Change buses at Bivio Polvica.
§Detours to Corsano and returns to Polvica.

6 Amalfi — Bomerano — San Lazzaro (for Agerola)

Amalfi	Bomerano	San Lazzaro	San Lazzaro	Bomerano	Amalfi
05.50	06.30	06.45	06.10*	06.25*	07.05*
07.45*	08.25*	08.40*	07.10	07.25	08.05
08.05*	08.45*		08.25**	08.40**	09.20**
08.45	09.25	09.40	08.40*	08.55*	09.35*
10.15	10.55	11.10	09.40	09.55	10.35
12.10*	12.50*			11.55*	12.35*
13.15*	13.55*	14.10*		13.20*	14.00*
14.00	14.40	14.55	13.10**	13.25**	14.05**
15.10*	15.50*	16.05*	14.10*	14.25*	15.05*
16.50	17.30	17.45	15.00	15.15	15.55
18.50*	19.30*	19.45*		16.00*	16.40*
20.50*	21.30*	21.45*	16.10*	16.25*	17.05*
			17.00*	17.15*	17.55*

* Not on Sundays and holidays
** Sundays and holidays only

17.50	18.10	18.45
19.50*	20.10*	20.45*

7 Positano — Monte Pertuso — Positano

Positano	Monte Pertuso	Positano
08.10	08.30	08.50
10.20	10.40	11.00
12.20	12.40	13.00
14.20	14.40	15.00
17.20	17.40	18.00
19.20	19.40	20.00

Notes

1 This service is operated by Positano town buses; purchase tickets on board.

2 Beyond Monte Pertuso, the bus continues on the road to Nocelle as far as current state of construction allows.

3 If travelling by bus along the coast road, connect with this service at 'Bivio Monte Pertuso' — where the mountain road leaves the coast road. This bus arrives here about 5min after departure from Positano centre (Piazza dei Mulini).

8 Sorrento — Massa Lubrense — Sant'Agata

Sorrento	Massa Lubrense	Bivio Titigliano	Sant' Agata	Sant' Agata	Bivio Titigliano	Massa Lubrense	Sorrento
06.05*	06.25*	06.30*	06.40*	05.20*	05.30*	05.35*	05.55*
06.45	07.05	07.10	07.20	06.00	06.10	06.15	06.35
07.25	07.45	07.50	08.00	06.40	06.50	06.55	07.15
07.55*	08.15*	08.20*	08.30*	07.20	07.30	07.35	08.00
08.15	08.35	08.40	08.50	07.45	07.55	08.00	08.20
08.50	09.10	09.15	09.25	08.45	08.55	09.00	09.20
09.15*	09.35*	09.40*	09.50*	09.15	09.25	09.30	09.50
09.40	10.00	10.05	10.15	10.15*	10.25*	10.30*	10.50*
10.10	10.30	10.35	10.45	10.40*	10.50*	10.55*	11.15*
11.05	11.25	11.30	11.40	11.15	11.25	11.30	11.50
12.15	12.35	12.40	12.50	12.00	12.10	12.15	12.35
12.45*	12.05*	12.10*	12.20*	13.00	13.10	13.15	13.35
13.05	13.25	13.30	13.40	13.40*	13.50*	13.55*	14.15*
13.30*	13.50*	13.55*	14.05*	14.20	14.30	14.35	14.55
13.50	14.10	14.15	14.25	15.10	15.20	15.25	15.45
14.25*	14.45*	14.50*	15.00*	16.00	16.10	16.15	16.35
15.10	15.30	15.35	15.45	17.10	17.20	17.25	17.45
16.10	16.30	16.35	16.45	18.00	18.10	18.15	18.35
17.05	17.25	17.30	17.40	19.00	19.10	19.15	19.35
18.10	18.30	18.35	18.45	19.50	20.00	20.05	20.25
19.00	19.20	19.25	19.35	20.35	20.45	20.50	21.10
19.50	20.10	20.15	20.25	21.15	21.25	21.30	21.50
20.45	21.05	21.10	21.20	22.05	22.15	22.20	22.40
21.25	21.45	21.50	22.00				
22.10	22.30	22.35	22.45				
22.50	23.10	23.15	23.25				

*Not on Sundays and holidays

Note: Bivio = turn-off to

Note: Capo lies between Sorrento and Massa Lubrense.

9 Sorrento — Massa Lubrense — Marina di Cantone

Sorrento	Massa Lubrense	Termini	Marina di Cantone	Marina di Cantone	Termini	Massa Lubrense	Sorrento
06.05*	06.25*	06.50*	07.05*	06.00*	06.15*	06.35*	06.55*
07.50	08.10	08.30	08.45		07.10*	07.30*	07.50*
10.45	11.05	11.25	11.40	07.05	07.20	07.35	07.55
11.40*	12.00*	12.15*	12.30	09.00	09.15	09.35	09.55
13.00*	13.20*	13.40*	13.55*	10.00**	10.15**	10.35**	10.55**
14.10*	14.30*	14.50*			12.10*	12.30*	12.50*
17.45	18.05	18.25	18.40	12.50*	13.05*	13.20*	13.40*
19.45	20.05	20.25	20.40		15.40*	16.00*	16.30
				18.20	18.35	18.55	19.15

*Not on Sundays and holidays
**Sundays and holidays only
Note: Nerano lies between Termini and Marina di Cantone; Capo lies between Sorrento and Massa Lubrense.

10 Sorrento — Sant'Agata — Marina di Cantone

Sorrento	Sant' Agata	Termini	Marina di Cantone	Marina di Cantone	Termini	Sant Agata	Sorrento
07.05	07.30					07.10	7.35
08.15	08.40					08.05	08.30
08.50	09.15	09.35	09.50			08.40*	09.05*
10.10	10.35	10.55	11.10			09.50	10.15
11.05	11.30					10.30	10.55
	12.00*	12.10*		10.15*	10.30*	10.40*	
12.10	12.35					11.35	12.00
13.05*	13.30*			11.20	11.35	11.45	
13.50	14.15	14.35	14.50	11.50	12.05	12.25	
	15.30*	15.50*	16.05*			12.55*	13.20*
	15.45**	15.55**	16.10**			13.20**	13.45**
16.10*	16.35*	16.55*	17.10*			13.30*	13.55*
17.05	17.30	17.50	18.05	14.05*	14.20*	14.40*	
18.10	18.35			14.55	15.10	15.30	15.55
19.30	19.55					16.30	16.55
20.45	21.10	21.30	21.45	16.15	16.30	16.50	17.15
						17.30	17.55
				17.20*	17.30*	17.45*	
						19.00	19.25
				18.50	19.05	19.25	
						20.10	20.35
				20.50	21.05	21.15	
				21.45	22.00	22.20	

*Not on Sundays and holidays
**Sundays and holidays only
Notes
1 Nerano lies between Termini and Marina Cantone.
2 Between Sorrento and Sant'Agata the bus takes the Nastro Azzurro road.

11 Sorrento — Fontanelle — Sant'Agata

Sorrento	Fontanelle	Sant'Agata	Sant'Agata	Fontanelle	Sorrento
06.40	07.00	07.10	07.15	17.25	07.45
08.20	08.40	08.50	08.55	09.05	09.25
10.00	10.20	10.30	10.35	10.45	11.05
11.20	11.40	11.50	11.55	12.05	12.25
13.00	13.20	13.30	13.35	13.45	14.05
14.30	14.50	15.00	15.05	15.15	15.35
16.20	16.40	16.50	16.55	17.05	17.25
18.20	18.40	18.50	18.55	19.05	19.25
20.15	20.35	20.45	20.45	20.55	21.15

Note: This service is operated by Circumvesuviana, leaving from Sorrento Station. Tickets need to be bought in tobbacconists or bars; SITA tickets are *not valid.*

12 Services on Capri

The service on the island is operated by Capri Buses. Purchase tickets on board, except on leaving Capri town, where there is a ticket office. Buses are relatively frequent. Routes:
Marina Grande — Capri
Marina Grande — Anacapri
Capri — Anacapri
Anacapri — Grotta Azzurra

13 Herculaneum (Ercolano) — Vesuvius

A year-round bus service is operated by SITA. Departs Ercolano railway station at 08.15, 10.20, 12.40 (tickets on bus). Departs the summit car park at 9.30, 11.30, 14.30, 16.30.

Price guidelines

Below are some typical fares, valid as of press date (winter 1995):

From the airport to Naples

    L3000 (airport bus)

    L1000 (yellow city bus No 14)

From Naples to your resort

    L3900 (Circumvesuviana railway) to Sorrento

    L6000 Sorrento (bus from Naples Airport to Piazza Tasso)

    L4500 Salerno (for Amalfi, Ravello, Maiori, Minori)

From Amalfi:

    L1500 Ravello, Maiori, Conca, Praiano, Pogerola

    L2000 Agerola, Erchie, Positano

    L2700 Salerno

    L3400 Sorrento

From Positano

    L1000 Monte Pertuso and Nocelle

From Maiori

    L1500 Polvica

    L2000 Capitignano

From Sorrento

    L1500 Massa Lubrense, Colli di San Pietro

    L2000 Sant'Agata, Termini, Nerano, Marina di Cantone, Positano

    L2700 Vèttica Maggiore, Praiano

    L3400 Amalfi

On Capri

    L1500 funicular from the Marina Grande up to the main town

    L1500 Capri to Anacapri, Capri to the Blue Grotto (Grotta Azzurra)

☀ **Index**

This index contains geographical names only. For other entries, see Contents, page 3. Page numbers in **bold** indicate a photograph; those in *italic* a town plan or an entry in a walk planner. Pronunciation guide: where a syllable in a place name is in **bold**, stress that syllable. Otherwise stress the next to last syllable (eg. A**mal**fi).

A country code for walkers and motorists

The experienced rambler is used to following a 'country code', but the tourist out for some fun may unwittingly cause damage, harm natural life or even endanger his own life. Rules for behaviour are important wherever people are free to roam over the countryside, and doubly so in some of the rugged or remote terrain of the Amalfi Coast, so please respect this code:

• **Do not light fires.** Woods may be tinder dry. Make sure your cigarettes are completely extinguished.

• **Protect all wild and cultivated plants.** Don't try to pick wild flowers or uproot saplings. They will die before you get them back to your hotel in any case.

• **Keep to the recognised paths** as described in this guide. If you find yourself going through a gateway, you are straying onto private land (except one gate on Walk segment 16).

• **Take all your litter back to your hotel with you.**

• **Do not damage walls or steps.**

• **Walkers — DO NOT TAKE RISKS!** This is the most important point of all. Some of the routes in this guide take you into rugged terrain or onto seldom-used paths. Should you have an accident you would be thrown onto your own resources to extricate yourself. So, weigh the risks clearly before walking alone. Always take enough equipment to cope with an unexpected enforced stop — extra food and clothing, a torch and a whistle, and especially plenty of water.

Sheep in the high farming area of Tramonti (Walk segment 43)